ARCHITECTURE FOR ART: AMERICAN ART MUSEUMS, 1938–2008

Architecture

for Art

AMERICAN ART MUSEUMS
1938–2008

Edited by Scott J. Tilden

Photography by Paul Rocheleau

Introduction by Wim de Wit

HARRY N. ABRAMS, INC., PUBLISHERS

EDITORIAL CONCEPT DEVELOPMENT
Richard Olsen
EDITOR
Barbara Burn
DESIGN
Henk van Assen with Amanda Bowers and Sarah Gifford
PRODUCTION MANAGER
Maria Pia Gramaglia

Library of Congress Cataloging-in-Publication Data

    Architecture for art : American art museums, 1938-2008 / edited by Scott J. Tilden ;
photography by Paul Rocheleau ; introduction by Wim de Wit.
        p. cm.
Includes bibliographical references and index.
ISBN 0-8109-4960-1 (hardcover)
1. Art museum architecture—United States. 2. Architecture—United States—20th century.
3. Architecture—United States—21st century. I. Tilden, Scott. II. Rocheleau, Paul.

NA6696.U6 A73 2004
727'.7'09730904—dc22

        2004001820

Printed and bound in China

The quotation from Frank Lloyd Wright reprinted on page 86 is copyrighted © 1960, 2004 by
    The Frank Lloyd Wright Foundation, Scottsdale, AZ.
The quotation from Louis I. Kahn reprinted on page 181 is copyrighted © 1977 by Yale University Press.

10 9 8 7 6 5 4 3 2 1

Harry N. Abrams, Inc.
100 Fifth Avenue
New York, N.Y. 10011
www.abramsbooks.com

Abrams is a subsidiary of

CONTENTS

Preface by Scott J. Tilden 7
Introduction by Wim de Wit 11

PREFACE

Scott J. Tilden

Once you could tell a lot about a community by its church. It was the place the city took pride in. Now it is the cultural center, the museum as monument.[1]
Philip Johnson, architect

In museums, the real challenge is to discover that perfect balance where the architecture and art enrich one another.[2]
Mario Botta, architect

Museums today are much larger physically as well as in size of staff and budgets than they were just a few decades ago. . . . The resulting pressures tend to lead to policies that are driven not by mission forces but by market forces. And when market forces dominate, the public's trust in museums will begin to erode.
Philippe de Montebello, director, The Metropolitan Museum of Art, New York

The United States truly suffers from an embarrassment of riches in regard to its art museums. Since 1970 more than six hundred new art museums have opened in this country, bringing the total to more than thirteen hundred.[4] Major art museums reported a growth in the 1990s of 113 percent in museum endowments, 483 percent in capital improvements, 50 percent in donated artwork, and 20 percent in museum attendance.[5] Nowhere was this prosperity more evident than in the creation of new museum buildings. These structures captured the public's imagination, stirred debate, and became one of the principal reasons for museum visits.

- Starting in 1938, with the Museum of Modern Art in New York, and continuing through the present day, museum directors and trustees have retained Modernist and contemporary architects to create structures with aesthetic values as significant as the collections they were designed to hold. These architects include Frank Gehry, Mario Botta, Marcel Breuer, I. M. Pei, Frank Lloyd Wright, Philip Johnson, Louis I. Kahn, Charles Gwathmey, Renzo Piano, Cesar Pelli, Ludwig Mies van der Rohe, Eliel Saarinen, Robert Venturi, Richard Meier, Rafael Viñoly, and Zaha Hadid. They designed museums that have become architectural icons, including the Guggenheim, Kimbell, Whitney, Getty, and the East Building of the National Gallery of Art.

- *Architecture for Art* chronicles this golden age of museum design and construction. What characterizes this period is not simply a large number of new or expanded museums by great architects, but a significant change in the mission of many American art museums. Like living organisms, museums have evolved and grown functionally more complex. America's art museums have expanded their missions and taken on new roles within their communities. They continue to address the aesthetic needs of their patrons. Many offer their visitors exhibitions of artworks from their permanent collections and access to blockbuster traveling exhibitions, which may range from Impressionist paintings to motorcycles. For a limited number of museums, the functions of collecting, preserving, and exhibiting art remain paramount and even exclusive.

- In 1970 Sebastian J. Adler Jr., founding director at the Contemporary Arts Museum Houston, described the genesis of the museum's straightforward design as a setting for changing exhibits. "We're going to dispense with a lot of unnecessary crap that most museums get stuck with. We don't need members' rooms and we don't need auditoriums and we don't need cafeterias. This museum cannot be either an acropolis or a country club and it won't be. It's going to be a place to move things—get 'em in and out—and it's going to be flexible enough so that it can function inside and out as an artistic medium in which artists can create imaginative works."[6]

- However most museums are now seeking to meet not only the aesthetic needs of their customers but also their dining, shopping, education, entertainment, and social needs. Journalist Andrew Marton comments, "These days, the average museum patron is almost as likely to gravitate towards the pleasures of an expertly prepared meal as to bask in the ineffable beauty of a Monet. . . . A seat at Bravo at the Museum of Fine Arts, Boston, is so prized that the museum keeps the restaurant open not only for the obvious lunch service but also for dinner three nights a week and for Sunday brunch."[7] The Modern Art Museum of Fort Worth offers its visitors outstanding cuisine and a lovely curved dining room overlooking

Corning Museum of Glass (photo by Andrew Fortune)

a reflecting pool. *Gourmet Magazine* selected its Café Moderne as one of the nation's best new restaurants last year.

• Museum stores, like those at the Metropolitan Museum of Art, have evolved from simple shops to elaborate emporiums. MoMA operates stores within its museum and separate shops in SoHo and on Fifty-third Street. The Corning Museum has devoted much of its patio-level floor to its retail stores known as GlassMarket and to its café and coffee bar. Corning Museum director David Whitehouse states, "The philosophy of the GlassMarket is to offer, in addition to souvenirs and household glassware, items that reflect our exhibits in the Art and History Galleries, like contemporary glass art, books, and videos, and our displays in the Innovation Center, like science-related items."

• Many art museums also provide the public with art, photography, and design classes; some even have affiliated schools such as the Corcoran College of Art + Design, which offers accredited degree programs. Museums routinely offer film series and evening and luncheon lectures. These cultural organizations rent out their spaces for meetings, birthdays, and corporate annual meetings. Some have even created junior trustee and auxiliary organizations to encourage the involvement of young professionals in the life of their museums. These men and women are attracted to the monthly wine and cheese parties to network and develop friendships as well as to view art. Museums have become what sociologist Ray Oldenburg calls "great good places." By this he means highly accessible and congenial settings outside the home and workplace where people feel welcome, find old and new friends, engage in conversation, and can purchase food and drink.[8] In describing his design for the Oakland Museum, Kevin Roche said, "The overwhelming concern was building a place where people could get together. It is really a community center as well as a museum."[9]

• Each of the above museum functions requires a shared or distinct space and represents a corresponding new design problem for the architect. Perhaps the most pressing problem confronting the architect of a museum today is how to generate a cutting-edge exterior design, which stimulates the imagination of the viewer. Neighboring hotels, businesses, and local governments often encourage museums to create buildings that appeal to tourists and residents. The main hall of Santiago Calatrava's new winged structure for the Milwaukee Art Museum houses few works of art but attracts thousands of patrons who visit its other galleries and local businesses. In addition to designing a striking façade, the architect must develop an interior plan with spaces that perform specific functions and meld into a coherent building. The difficulties are multiplied if the architect has to work with existing structures and create new wings.

Museum of Fine Arts, Boston (photo by Paul Rocheleau)

In *Towards a New Museum*, Victoria Newhouse dedicates a complete chapter to these challenges in "Wings That Don't Fly (And Some That Do)." Controversy surrounds plans that call for tearing down and replacing existing museum structures. The Los Angeles County Museum of Art eventually set aside Rem Koolhaas's 2001 plans for a radical makeover of its campus due to financial and public pressures.

• *Architecture for Art* documents the evolution of museum missions, functions, and design over a seventy-year period. It explores the exceptional architecture of thirty-nine American art museums located in cities and small towns. (A number of other museums would have been included, but they chose not to participate.) The book begins in 1938 with the creation of the MoMA and ends in 2008 with the completion of the expansion of the Corcoran Gallery of Art. Selection criteria included: quality of design, geographic breadth, and span of styles from Modernist to Post-Modern and beyond.

• In the introduction that follows this preface, Wim de Wit, special collections head of the Getty Research Institute and the author of numerous architectural books and articles, describes the social and historical context for the architecture of American art museums. Equally important is his examination of the central debate on contemporary museum design. Does the architect create a neutral white space where art is exhibited? Or does the architect develop a design that not only meets the functional requirements but also is noteworthy from an artistic standpoint?

• Paul Rocheleau conceived the idea for this book, after visiting the Des Moines Art Center and being impressed by the superb buildings by Eliel Saarinen, I. M. Pei, and Richard Meier. Mr. Rocheleau invited me to join him on the venture, and I enthusiastically agreed. He faced the daunting task of conveying through a limited number of photographs the design and beauty of these buildings, each of which merits a complete book. He has captured splendid images of the art museums.

• The inspiration for this book's text format came from Helen Searing's catalogue *New American Art Museums*, published in association with an exhibition at the Whitney Museum of American Art in 1982. For each museum, this book provides critical reviews and statements by the museum director and architect on the collections, programs, and buildings. I chose to adopt this format because I wanted to create a book with multiple voices of directors, architects, scholars, and critics.

• Paul Rocheleau and I wish to thank those people who helped make this book possible. Our acquiring editor, Richard Olsen, believed in this book from its earliest conception. Our editor, Barbara Burn, shared her extensive knowledge of museums and publishing with us and shaped the vision and text of this book. Our designer, Henk van Assen, created a book that unifies word and image and beautifully reveals its themes. Our publisher, Eric Himmel, had the courage to expand the book beyond its original scope and specifications and realize its full potential.

• We could not have created this book without the cooperation and participation of architects, museum directors, their assistants, and museum public relations, rights and reproductions, security, and curatorial staffs. We want to express our sincere appreciation to these men and women as well as to those critics and scholars whose writings help illuminate our understanding of the buildings included in this book.

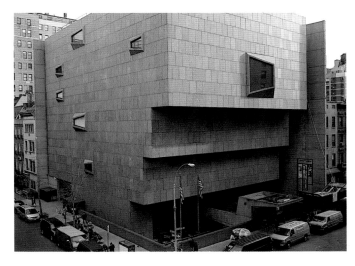

Whitney Museum of American Art (photo by Scott J. Tilden)

1   Philip Johnson, as quoted in Douglas Davis, "The Museum Explosion," *Newsweek* (September 17, 1973), pp. 88–89.

2   Mario Botta, "Architect's Statement," see page 166.

3   Philippe de Montebello, "How Museums Risk Losing Public Trust," *Whose Muse: Art Museums and Public Trust* (Princeton, Princeton University Press, 2004).

4   Victoria Newhouse, *Towards a New Museum* (New York: Monacelli Press, 1998), inside cover, and Suzanne Loebl, *America's Art Museums: A Traveler's Guide to Great Collections Large and Small* (New York: W. W. Norton, 2002), p. 23.

5   Association of Art Museum Directors, *Survey State of the Nation's Art Museums*, (AAMD, 2002), pp. 2–3.

6   Jay Jacobs, "A Commitment to the Future: Adler of the CAM," *Art Gallery* (May 1970).

7   Andrew Marton, *The News-Times* (December 31, 2003).

8   Ray Oldenburg, *The Great Good Place* (New York: Marlowe & Company, 1999).

9   Kevin Roche, quoted in Douglas Davis, "The Museum Explosion," p. 89.

Solomon R. Guggenheim Museum (photo by Scott J. Tilden)

WHEN MUSEUMS WERE WHITE
A STUDY OF THE MUSEUM AS BUILDING TYPE [1]

Wim de Wit

In the early 1980s, a group of Los Angeles collectors interested in contemporary art took the initiative to establish a museum dedicated exclusively to the collection and display of contemporary art. They raised $23 million, found a downtown site on Bunker Hill in a new development of offices, stores, apartment buildings, and hotels, and hired the eminent Japanese architect Arata Isozaki to design the new museum. Ground was broken in late 1983 and construction was expected to take about three years. However, the museum staff, led first by Pontus Hulten and very soon thereafter by Richard Koshalek, did not want to wait three years to organize their first exhibition. Instead, in a conscious attempt to sustain the excitement and momentum created during the initial fund drive, they decided to open a temporary museum as soon as possible in two old industrial buildings in an area known as Little Tokyo, just east of downtown Los Angeles. Renovated by the then-not-yet-so-well-known architect Frank Gehry, the Temporary Contemporary, as it was called at the time (now the Geffen Contemporary), was an instant success. Visitors liked its informality and unpretentiousness: people felt, and still feel, at home in the huge open spaces that seem to have no design to them; they feel comfortable with the open trusses under the roof that are not hidden by a dropped ceiling; and they admire Gehry's trademark steel and chain-link canopy, which marks the entrance. In short, it is the seeming absence of design that has made the building so popular.

• Isozaki's Museum of Contemporary Art (MOCA) building did not elicit an equally positive reception when it opened in late 1986. A review of the literature suggests that, although the museum trustees wanted a famous architect to design their building, they were somewhat uneasy about what might result. They wanted a building that, at least inside, would be totally neutral: clean, white rooms that would respect the art to be displayed there. Christopher Knight remarked in the *Los Angeles Herald Examiner* that crucial decisions about such matters were not made without friction, although in the end "a compromise had been successfully reached: complete 'neutrality' inside, complete Isozaki-style articulation outside." [2]

• Given these constraints, Isozaki's solution appears truly masterful. In order to have little impact on the surrounding high-rise hotels, apartments, and office towers—and to avoid being overwhelmed by them—most of the museum is built underground (actually, inside and on top of a large parking garage on Bunker Hill). Only a small part of the galleries projects above street level. Elements such as curatorial offices, the bookstore, and the library are in a separate building above ground, which also serves to mark the entrance into the building complex. Despite its thoughtful design, the MOCA building never achieved the popularity of the Temporary Contemporary building. In most accounts, the architect was criticized either because he had done too much or because he had not done enough.

• These responses to two related buildings testify to the complexity of a problem faced by every architect and museum director—namely, what role can or should architectural design play in the production of an art museum space? Can the architect, who is as much an artist as any sculptor or painter, be permitted to create a building that incorporates his or her ideas of what museum architecture can and should be, or should personal vision be relinquished in favor of a box in which art can be displayed to best advantage? Does architectural expression tend to overwhelm art, or can architecture and art coexist and complement each other? These questions have been asked repeatedly in the last three decades in relation to many museums, ranging from the Solomon R. Guggenheim Museum in New York by Frank Lloyd Wright to the San Francisco Museum of Modern Art by Mario Botta, to name just two examples.

• To those with a passing interest in the subject of museum architecture, it may seem that this conundrum has been around as long as museums have been in existence, but this is a misconception. In fact, the issue has a shorter pedigree, having been raised to prominence only in the years since Modernism was introduced in museum architecture, in the middle of the twentieth century. Modernist structures of steel, glass, and whitewashed concrete were considered sufficiently neutral to allow for the

showing of any kind of art, and this formal vocabulary was so strong that for a time no other kind of museum environment could be imagined. But changes in the physical characteristics of the works of art displayed by museums have also contributed greatly to the development of a new attitude with regard to museum architecture. In order to appreciate the reasons for this change, it is helpful to examine the history of the museum as building type.

• As many recent studies of the history of collecting and display have shown, museums evolved in the second half of the eighteenth century from collections of art objects or collections of curiosa originally housed in private settings and subsequently made accessible to a larger public. Noble or royal families, influenced by enlightened thinking of the time, concentrated their often vast collections in a refurbished palace or villa and opened them to the public, sharing their wealth without actually relinquishing any personal property. Architecturally, these early museums retained their original residential character, although the rooms themselves might be lavishly redecorated to create an appropriate setting for the art and to reflect the importance of the family that owned this art.

• Diverse collections of works of art were opened up everywhere in Europe, the most famous of which was probably the Louvre in Paris. However, among princely palaces and their collections, the Villa Borghese in Rome is perhaps more revealing of how architectural solutions were achieved and what role was played by the architect in that process. The paintings and sculpture in the Villa Borghese were originally assembled in the early seventeenth century as a semipublic collection by Cardinal Scipione Borghese, a nephew of Pope Paul V. The collection was converted into a public museum in the 1780s and 1790s by Prince Marcantonio Borghese, who hired architect Antonio Asprucci and his son, Mario Asprucci, among others, to transform the villa's rooms into galleries. Each hall was decorated in a style understood as supportive of the art objects to be shown in it: ceilings were decorated with large paintings, doors were surrounded by heavy frames, and wall surfaces were subdivided into smaller framed panels containing mural paintings or sculptural reliefs. Fear that the art on display would be overwhelmed by the decoration of the walls does not appear to have been a major concern.

• Over the course of the next century and a half, the palatial buildings housing these collections became extremely influential in the development of the museum building as a type. Long corridors with adjacent spacious rooms were deemed appropriate for the display of paintings and sculpture in chronological order and organized by school; each group of artists could be shown in its own room. The Louvre was one of the earliest museums in which the building's spatial layout lent itself to such a didactic display. As Carol Duncan noted in her book *Civilizing Rituals: Inside*

Public Art Museums: "In a relatively short time, the Louvre's directors (drawing partly on German and Italian precedents) worked out a whole set of practices that came to characterize art museums everywhere. In short, the museum organized its collections into art-historical schools and installed them so as to make visible the development and achievement of each school."[3]

• The Louvre was also influential with regard to another important feature of museum design: the lighting of the galleries. It was in this building that architects and those responsible for the installation of the works of art first experimented with light entering the rooms from above, through skylights. Lighting in a museum building, like acoustics in a concert hall, is one of the determining factors for the functional success of the space. For that reason, the issue of gallery illumination remains almost as controversial as the role of architectural expression in a space devoted to the exhibition of works of art.

• During the nineteenth century, the Louvre became a general prototype for museum architecture, thanks to the work of J. N. L. Durand, architectural theoretician and professor who recommended to his students the ideal floor plan for a museum building that showed many similarities to the Louvre—a huge, square block with long corridors running along the perimeter and giving access to relatively small rooms. Inside this square was a Greek cross built up similarly of corridors and small galleries, and at the center of the cross, and thus the center of the museum, was a circular space covered by a dome. The four courtyards created by the cross inside the square were kept uncovered. This plan had enormous appeal for the architectural world because of its symmetry—an organizing feature typical of most Beaux-Arts designs of the nineteenth and early twentieth centuries—and because of the modularity of the design, which meant that the large square block could easily be divided into half blocks or quarter blocks according to the funds available, while keeping the option open for additional parts to be built later.

• This museum type can be found all over the world, but it became especially popular in the United States, where most of the museums built in the late nineteenth and early twentieth centuries were designed by Beaux-Arts–trained architects. Examples range from the Museum of Fine Arts, Boston (Guy Lowell, 1909), to the Cleveland Museum of Art (Hubbell and Benes, 1916) and the National Gallery of Art in Washington, D.C. (John Russell Pope, 1941). Even the Corcoran Gallery in Washington (Ernest Flagg, 1893–95), despite its regular site plan, is laid out according to this principle. One of the last museums in this series is the Solomon R. Guggenheim Museum in New York (1943–59) in which Frank Lloyd Wright, as indicated by Helen Searing in her book *New American Art Museums*,[4] posed the Beaux-Arts circular atrium space as the essence of the museum

Gallery, Isozaki's MOCA at California Plaza
(photo by Paul Rocheleau)

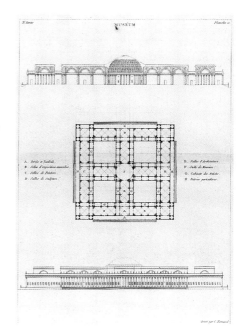

J. N. L. Durand's prototype museum plan

Kimbell Art Museum (photo by Paul Rocheleau)

building and constructed the surrounding processional display spaces as a single spiraling ramp rising above the central void. By placing the gallery spaces on the ramp along the perimeter of the atrium space, Wright made the visitor's progress through his museum even more linear than any of the Beaux-Arts museum buildings ever could have done.

• The interiors of these classically laid out museums were moderately decorated: there might be a frieze along the upper part of a wall or a molding around a wall surface in order to frame the pieces to be hung on that wall, but the design is generally quite sober. By the mid-twentieth century, however, museums all over Europe and the United States were virtually whitewashed as the culmination of a trend to modernize both museum practice and the display environment. The museum's original function of storeroom-cum-gallery of art, where amateur and specialist alike could study art history, was under increasing pressure as the museum gradually developed into a place where curators were no longer caretakers but scholars with expertise in a specific period or aspect of the history of art. For a variety of reasons, scholar-curators saw their task as educating the public through temporary exhibitions on specialized topics. Exhibition galleries were no longer static spaces in which the same works of art were shown year after year, and museums now required flexible spaces without ornamentation that might be appropriate to one exhibition but clash with the next. The generally accepted classical layout of the art museum plan needed to be rethought and revised.

• Alfred Lichtwark, director of the Kunsthalle in Hamburg, was one of several theoreticians who wrote about the need to reconceptualize the museum building. Lichtwark had pointed out in the early 1910s that not only was a new architecture being developed without the usual references to historic styles, but the function of the museum was also changing. Clearly influenced by rationalist thinking about architecture, he promoted a museum building that would be designed according to its function rather than according to a pre-existing building type. Lichtwark's ideal museum consisted of long corridors that would function as thoroughfares and exhibition halls that could be entered from these corridors, thus separating the function of movement through a building from that of contemplating works of art. For lighting of the galleries, Lichtwark preferred windows rather than skylights, but under no circumstance could the placement of the windows be determined by the composition of the façade, which should take shape as an envelope around a functional arrangement of spaces and windows. The windows should be so placed as to achieve optimal results in the galleries; that is, they should leave ample space for the works of art on the walls and be placed sufficiently high in the gallery to illuminate the entire room.

• Modernist architects of the early twentieth century must have felt comfortable with Lichtwark's proposals, which applied widely recognized Modernist principles to replace the traditional type of museum building. Perhaps the most important new art museum building of the period between the two world wars was the Museum of Modern Art in New York, completed in 1939 according to the design of Philip L. Goodwin and Edward Durell Stone. Both outside and inside, the architects of the MoMA building adhered strictly to the practices of Modernism as far as colors and materials were concerned; white walls, glass, and steel were abundantly present. The exhibition galleries were relatively small, which allowed for close-up viewing of the works of art, a characteristic that the museum has managed to retain over the years. Even in the expansion that is currently being constructed according to the design of Japanese architect Yoshio Taniguchi, this intimacy will to a large extent be maintained. MoMA has become the guardian of high Modernism and its building is the physical expression of this endeavor.

• A significant change in museum design was catalyzed after World War II by developments in the sphere of commercial galleries and museums of modern art, which required spaces conducive to the display of ever larger paintings and pieces of sculpture. As the art market expanded and diversified, exhibition spaces had to become flexible to allow for a great variety of displays. The economy of managing museums also changed considerably. In order to attract a broad public, museums began to organize popular thematic displays, which cost a great deal of money and required active fund-raising campaigns, as well as public amenities such as restaurants and shops. Potential donors (of both funds and collections) were persuaded that museums were worth supporting and expanding to satisfy the growing audience.

• Although the white unadorned gallery was now unequivocally accepted, the preferred layout was no longer clear. Museums were designed to have big, open halls that allowed for people to move through easily and that could house works of art from different periods and of different dimensions. One of the most effective designs was that of Louis Kahn for the Kimbell Art Museum in Fort Worth, Texas (1966–72). In order to accommodate the relatively small works of art in the Kimbell's collection, Kahn brought the scale of the exhibition space down by dividing the building into a series of vaulted spaces placed parallel to one another. The vaults define gallery spaces that are comprehensible and therefore manageable for the viewer, but since there are no walls in between most of the vaulted spaces, the galleries can also be read as large open spaces that allow for great flexibility. Kahn managed to give the museum perfect proportions so that the art does not look overwhelmed by the architecture, which certainly has a presence of its own and does not disappear

Milwaukee Art Museum (photo by Paul Rocheleau)

in the background. The natural light coming into the gallery spaces from above through narrow slits that follow the curve of the vaults makes the Kimbell one of the most beautiful museum spaces designed in the twentieth century.

• About the time that the Kimbell reached completion, a new museum in Paris—the Centre Pompidou (1972–77)—created a huge stir because of its appearance, both on the outside and in the galleries. The design of this museum aimed at flexibility achieved by architecturally turning the building inside out. All structural, architectural, and utilitarian elements, such as stairs, columns, ducts and pipes, were removed from the interior and became the building's exterior. As a result, the architects could create large, undivided floors inside with hardly any interruption of spatial flow. The building became wildly popular among tourists, although most visitors to the building did not actually visit the exhibitions,[5] choosing instead to ride the escalators on the museum's exterior. Staff and exhibition visitors, however, did not feel comfortable in the building's enormous exhibition spaces, where noise levels are high and exposed structural elements are often experienced as intrusive as well as hostile to the viewing of the art. As an example of urban design, however, the museum was a huge success. The square in front of the museum became a gathering point for the young and hip; and the dilapidated Beaubourg neighborhood, which had housed Les Halles, the nineteenth-century meat and fish market, attracted numerous galleries and stores with merchandise for tourists. Thanks to this one building, a huge area in Paris was revived.

• The success of the Centre Pompidou brought about a new round of museum buildings. Every city that aspired to a place in the worlds of culture and mass tourism built at least one museum in the ensuing decades. A great deal has been written about the place of the museum in modern society. The idea that the museum now plays the role that the cathedral did in earlier times, that it is a place where people gather in surroundings expressing their cultural ideals, can be found in many studies of the museum in the late twentieth century. Victoria Newhouse in her book *Towards a New Museum* described this development as part of a trend in which entertainment governs every experience.[6] Although I concur, I believe we need to take the analysis one step further. Television, videos, DVDs, and amusement parks have encouraged people to demand constant visual stimulation. Every waiting room, check-in line, or other place where people have to spend time and may get bored is now equipped with a television monitor. People expect to be entertained. At the same time, they have also become visually sophisticated and are no longer likely to be excited about a whitewashed room with works of art on the wall or documents in a case. Exhibition design has become as innovative as the products of the entertainment industry, and the architectural

design of the museum buildings has become equally important for the visual experience.

• Museum boards and city governments have gone in search of well-known architects who can give a city a "monument" that will attract not only the large crowds who want to see art in an exciting environment, but also the ever-growing groups of people with a passionate interest in modern architecture. A museum that makes a stunning architectural statement can become a tourist attraction and revive the economy of a city or region. As a result, the architectural envelope of a museum is now as important as the art inside. The old question—can architecture and art co-exist?—seems to have been resolved. At least, people seem to have accepted that in order for a museum to function well, its architecture has to be as strong as the works of art it contains. An architectural design that stands out individually is therefore more important than a design that fits within the guidelines of a building type. No one now expects an architect to follow specific rules set by a building typology. And gallery spaces are no longer necessarily huge rectangular cubes but can take on virtually any shape. Although most galleries are still white inside, even that common element is up for discussion.

• The best-known museum of this new era is Frank Gehry's Guggenheim Museum in Bilbao. But there are others of great merit, as this book will demonstrate. Santiago Calatrava's addition to the Milwaukee Art Museum (1994–2001)—a museum wing containing a gallery for temporary exhibitions, two sculpture galleries, a store, an auditorium, and an exhibition pavilion—is probably one of the most prominent examples of the "museum as urban monument." Intended to make an existing museum (designed in the mid-1950s by Eliel and Eero Saarinen, and expanded twenty years later by a local firm) into a landmark provocative enough to draw people from all over the world, Calatrava's wing has certainly made its mark. In order to protect the art objects on display in the exhibition pavilion, the architect placed two gigantic, movable sun shades over the glass dome that covers the pavilion. When these shades open up, they look like the wings of a bird, or perhaps like the tail of a giant whale plunging into Lake Michigan. The shades have a functional raison d'être, but their impact encompasses more than their function. They will become like the Eiffel Tower of Milwaukee, a silhouette that one will see reproduced everywhere.

• Although it is still too soon to be sure, two recent museum designs offer solutions that may have broader applications. The Rosenthal Center for Contemporary Art in Cincinnati, by Zaha Hadid (1998–2003), and Diller and Scofidio's design for the Institute of Contemporary Art in Boston (currently in design) are both urban monuments, but they are not isolated as such. Instead, they aim to relate to their urban environment and have galleries that coexist well with the art on display. Both designs strive for a smooth transition from the street into the building and from there into the galleries. Hadid speaks of an urban carpet that starts on the street, continues into the lobby, and transforms into the back wall at the far end of that space. Via ramps located in the back of the building, one reaches the various galleries that on each floor fan out from the ramps. The circulation is impeccable. In Diller and Scofidio's design for the Boston museum, the street changes gradually into steps that at first act as bleachers from which one can view the harbor and continues inside as a theater. In the back of the theater, the steps turn into the rear wall, which then continues into the floor of an 18,000-square-foot column-free exhibition space, which is wrapped in transparent and translucent glass. One will be aware at all times of the presence of the harbor right outside the museum.

• The history of the museum as a building type reflects developments similar to those in other types, such as schools, libraries, movie theaters, and even churches. The nineteenth-century need to classify and create visually distinct building types for various community functions became obsolete in the years following World War II. Modernist architects preferred to give expression to the function of a building by wrapping façades tightly around carefully laid-out floor plans, not by working with a prescribed spatial arrangement to tell the viewer what happened inside. The classical ornament used to signify a building's purpose had lost its meaning, although signage (carved in stone or placed on banners) became an important means for informing passers-by what takes place inside. It is impossible to know if the need for building types will eventually return, but recent examples suggest that some architects and curators want to devise gallery spaces in which the art and architecture together create a total environment, conducive to contemplation of the ideas behind the art on display. It will be interesting to see if this trend takes root.

1   This is a modified version of an article with the same title first published in an exhibition catalogue published to accompany an exhibition organized by the Univeristy of Southern California's Museum Studies Program: Selma Holo, Katrina Ampil Bagaybagayan, et al., *Open House West: Museum Architecture and Changing Civic Identity* (Los Angeles: Fisher Gallery, USC, 1999), pp. 12–19. I wish to thank Catherine Butler for the assistance she provided to my research, and—as always—my wife, Nancy J. Troy, for her critical support and advice.

2   Christopher Knight, "MOCA Unveils Latest Design for Bunker Hill Museum," *Los Angeles Herald Examiner* (1981), n.p.

3   Carol Duncan, *Civilizing Rituals: Inside Public Art Museums* (London/New York: Routledge, 1995), p. 24.

4   Helen Searing, *New American Art Museums* (New York: Whitney Museum of Art, in association with the University of California Press, 1982), pp. 53–56. See also "The Development of a Museum Typology" in *Museum News*, vol. 65, no. 4 (1987), pp. 20–31, by the same author.

5   One should note here that the museum is only one of several tenants, including a library, auditorium, restaurant, and bar, each of which attracts their own visitors.

6   Victoria Newhouse, *Towards a New Museum* (New York: Monacelli Press, 1998), pp. 190–92. It is still too early to say how the light levels will be controlled, and how the art will be hung in this wide-open space.

Contemporary Arts Center, Cincinnati (photo by Paul Rocheleau)

MUSEUMS

AMERICAN FOLK ART
MUSEUM NEW YORK, NY

Tod Williams / Billie Tsien

MUSEUM DIRECTOR'S STATEMENT

A small group of enthusiasts founded the American Folk Art Museum on June 23, 1961. Sharing the conviction that folk art was a vital element in American cultural history, the founders of the museum aspired to establish a national center in the city of New York for its study and appreciation. Opening its doors to the public for the first time on September 27, 1963, the museum initially occupied the rented parlor floor of a townhouse at 49 West Fifty-third Street in Manhattan.

▪ In Europe, where the term originated, ethnographers define "folk art" as the tradition-bound arts of peasant communities. In America, however, the study of folk art has grown within less-well-defined boundaries. Rather than placing their principal emphasis on class and tradition, American art historians have tended to locate the terrain of folk art in the work of artists who come to their creative expression from outside the formal systems or institutions of the art world. Instead, they focus on artists whose training for the most part is in an informal or nonacademic setting, or who are self-taught. The multifaceted mission of the American Folk Art Museum is tied to this understanding of the field.

▪ The first object to enter the museum's collection was the now famous *Flag Gate* (c. 1876), a gift to the institution in 1962 from Herbert W. Hemphill Jr., a founding trustee and influential pioneer collector in the field. Since then the museum's holdings have grown to encompass more than 4,000 objects in various mediums, including the highly important collection formed by Ralph Esmerian, president of the museum's board from 1977 to 1999 and chairman since then. Among the major works of art in the museum's collection is Ammi Phillips's great portrait, *Girl in Red Dress with Her Cat and Dog* (c. 1830). The Contemporary Center is devoted to the collection, exhibition, and study of the work of twentieth- and twenty-first-century self-taught artists from the United States and abroad; a recent acquisition is the complete archives of and twenty-four paintings by the Chicago artist Henry Darger.

▪ After operating in a succession of inadequate spaces for many years, the museum commissioned Tod Williams / Billie Tsien & Associates to design a 30,000-square-foot structure at 45 West Fifty-third Street in New York City. Inaugurated on December 11, 2001, four decades after the establishment of the institution, the museum's new home includes exhibition galleries, library, auditorium, classroom, shop, café, and offices, among other facilities.

Gerard C. Wertkin

ARCHITECT'S STATEMENT

This new eight-level museum on Fifty-third Street in New York City devotes the four upper floors to gallery space for permanent and temporary exhibitions. A skylight above a grand stair allows natural light to filter into the galleries and lower levels through openings at each floor.

▪ Places for the showing of art are built into the structure and circulation paths of the building, using a series of niches so that visitors will encounter art in unexpected and informal settings. The experience of the museum visitor is a somewhat idiosyncratic and personal journey through the use of multiple paths of movement. We believe that it is more like a house for folk art rather than a typical museum. Thus, there are several "surprise" staircases that allow visitors alternate ways to descend from floor to floor. This project presents the museum's collections and exhibitions by creating an environment for both frequent and first-time visitors that is amazing and memorable.

▪ At the mezzanine level, a small café overlooking Fifty-third Street has a dramatic view of the two-story atrium. The building extends two levels underground: one floor holds the new auditorium and classroom facilities, while the lowest level houses museum offices, a library, and an archive. At the entrance level is a museum store, with access during non-museum hours via a separate door.

▪ The façade of the American Folk Art Museum is designed to make a strong but quiet statement of independence. It is sculptural in form, recalling an abstracted open hand and folds slightly inward to create a faceted plane. Metal panels of Tombasil clad the building. These panels will catch the glow of the morning and early evening sun as it rises and sets, east and west along Fifty-third Street.

Billie Tsien, Tod Williams / Billie Tsien & Associates

First floor, north gallery

AWARDS

- Arup Best Building in the World 2002, *World Architecture Magazine*
- Municipal Art Society Masterworks Award, 2002
- Brendan Gill Award, 2002
- NYC AIA Award, 2002
- National AIA Award, 2003

CRITICS' COMMENTS

The Bilbao Effect—a worldwide frenzy for museum architecture as a tourist destination and a public spectacle rather than as a home for art—has spiraled so far out of control that some corrective was desperately needed.... A superlative alternative to that alarming trend is happily at hand in the new American Folk Art Museum. Its intelligent equipoise between architectural excitement and genuine attentiveness to the works of art that it displays is exemplary, as is its equally appropriate balance between physical grandeur and spiritual intimacy.
Martin Filler, *The New Republic* (January 14, 2002)

The architects Tod Williams and Billie Tsien faced a daunting challenge: putting a $22 million building on a tiny plot, 40 feet wide, and nearly surrounded by a cultural behemoth—the construction site for the $650 million mega-expansion of the Museum of Modern Art.... But they took advantage of the small scale to make something elegant, intricate, and memorable.
Cathleen McGuigan, *Newsweek* (January 21, 2002)

Left: Façade
Opposite left: Permanent gallery stairwell with window into exhibition area
Opposite above right: Southwest corner of Wilkerson galleries
Opposite below right: Second floor, northeast gallery

AMON CARTER MUSEUM

Philip Johnson / Alan Ritchie

MUSEUM DIRECTOR'S STATEMENT

Amon G. Carter's lifetime of philanthropy grew out of his humble beginnings and self-made rise to success. Although born in a log cabin in Texas, he amassed a fortune as an entrepreneur and was for many years Fort Worth's most ardent champion. He also acquired a major collection of American art. To house his collection, his will provided for the establishment of a free public museum devoted to American art—a museum he would never see.

- After Carter's death in 1955, the Amon G. Carter Foundation and members of his family called upon the architect Philip Johnson to create a museum building. Visualizing what he termed a "timeless classicism," Johnson designed an elegantly styled structure with a portico that afforded a broad view of downtown Fort Worth. Inside the building, Johnson arranged a series of identical galleries emanating from a large open space that rose to the full height of the building. The museum opened to the public on January 21, 1961.

- Although the museum's collections and programs evolved over the following decades, its physical spaces did not keep pace. By 1995 the permanent collection numbered nearly a quarter-million objects and included one of the country's most important collections of photographs. As a result, plans were approved for a new expansion. Philip Johnson again became involved and developed a design for a new structure directly behind the original building. It would be sheathed in dark brown Arabian granite, providing an appealing contrast to the 1961 edifice.

- The museum closed to the public in August 1999, and over the next twenty-two months Johnson's design was implemented. The increase of nearly 90,000 square feet has allowed the museum to display more than four times as many artworks from its famed collections. Other new features include a 160-seat auditorium with advanced Internet and distance-learning technology; a major research library with enhanced facilities; sophisticated climate-controlled spaces for care of the art collection, including both cool and cold storage for photography; a greatly expanded museum store; and a new conservation laboratory for photographs and works on paper.

- The Amon Carter Museum is now able to exhibit the full breadth of its permanent collection on a rotating basis and to serve as a venue for major traveling exhibitions. It is a fitting tribute to Amon G. Carter and his vision for the community he loved. The museum that bears his name is part of the heritage of Texas and an active contributor to the cultural life of the nation.

Rick Stewart

ARCHITECT'S STATEMENT

The Amon Carter Museum, designed by Philip Johnson, first opened its doors in 1961. The two-story building, clad in fossilized shell stone quarried locally in Austin, sits at the top of a series of stepped terraces with sweeping views back to downtown Fort Worth. The beautiful double-height pavilion with its arched portico façade forms the main entrance to the museum and has become a city landmark. In 1964 and again in 1977, additions to the building were constructed west of the existing museum, adhering to the design and materials of the original structure.

- Although these additions preserved the terraced lawns and landscaping in front of the museum, they offered only a minimal increase in gallery space. In 1997 Philip Johnson and I were consulted regarding the fresh challenge of a major expansion to the museum. We suggested that an entirely new addition, preserving only the 1961 building, should be considered if the museum desired world-class galleries for its ever-increasing collections. With the museum's endorsement, we proceeded with our design, adding nearly 90,000 square feet in the triangular-shape site behind the pavilion. This provided two floors of public space with nearly four times the exhibition area and three levels of administration, education, conservation, and storage facilities. For the exterior, we moved away from the use of the cream-color shell stone and instead selected rich brown granite of very even texture, quarried in Saudi Arabia. The result is an elegant juxtaposition of color, as the new building establishes a complementary and effective backdrop to the original. An additional entrance was incorporated into the Lancaster Avenue side of the new structure. There, visitors enter a new double-height atrium, where a grand staircase leads to the main galleries. The lower galleries, shop, auditorium, and library are on the ground level, with both floors connected to the original building.

- Natural light enters the atrium indirectly through the sides of the great lantern hovering above. The quality and color of the Texas light make the atrium a natural orientation point for visitors throughout the museum. To unite this space with the original building, the interior surfaces of the atrium consist of the same Texas shell stone, extruded bronze, and pink-and gray-flecked Maine granite found in the 1961 structure. The patron of the project was the same as in the 1960s, Ruth Carter Stevenson, daughter of the museum's founder. We credit Mrs. Stevenson for her leadership in successfully remaking this important Texas institution.

Alan Ritchie, Philip Johnson/Alan Ritchie Architects

East façade

Opposite: Gallery in east-entrance lobby
Above: South gallery, looking north through atrium
Left: Colonnade on east façade

Opposite: North galleries

Above left: Main entrance to new addition

Above right: Atrium and south entrance lobby below and south gallery above

BELLEVUE ART MUSEUM

Steven Holl

MUSEUM DIRECTOR'S STATEMENT

Bellevue Art Museum (BAM) is a bold, brave statement—in its architecture, program-ming, and as testimony to community support. Steven Holl's high ceilings, curved walls, and expansive floor space are powerful assets that welcome strong exhibition design and large-scale sculpture, design, and architecture exhibitions, as well as site-specific interventions. Art needs to work and play with his building. Our goal is to alter the look and focus of the museum's three floors and external spaces every three to four months. Strategies include powerful wall colors, art that flies from ceiling to floor, and spaces that go from darkness to full light. Visitors have the experience of five to six different installations at any one time.

- Although attention is paid to color, light, scale, and flow, content is central. BAM's main focus is contemporary art with strong ties to modern art. Our modern and contem-porary program extends beyond art to include design, architecture, and craft. In addition, BAM is strongly committed to working with living Northwest artists, especially through site-specific interventions. Our program calls for innovatively presented exhibitions that are set in social, historical, and cultural contexts; rich in visual interest, content, and quality; attractive to strong regional and national attention and support; multidisci-plinary in scope; and complementary to the museum's education programming.

- It is more or less clear what the Pacific Northwest is known for in terms of art— ceramics, glass, and a school of painting. BAM is passionate about taking a leadership role in encouraging regional talent and pushing experimental, adventuresome work in mediums ranging from ceramics to industrial design to new media. The question of interest to BAM is: what will the area be known for in the future and how can we be a vital catalyst in its realization?

Kathleen Harleman

ARCHITECT'S STATEMENT

The Bellevue Art Museum maintains no permanent collection but rather collaborates with local arts and educational institutions to provide innovative arts programming and changing temporary exhibitions. As an "art garage" open to the street, the muse-um provides a new pedestrian city scale at the center of Bellevue, as well as an active workshop for new art projects.

- Tripleness is the organizing concept for the building. A non-dialectic openness of experience, thought, and contact give character to space on three levels, in three gal-leries, with three different light conditions and three circulation options. BAM's spirit of openness is expressed in the three main lofts, which are each slightly warped and gripped by the end wall structures. The outer walls, in a special "shot crete," support the inner lightweight steel framework. The three distinct lighting conditions of the three gallery lofts are analogous to three different conditions of time and light. Linear, ongoing time is expressed in the evenness of the light in the north loft; cyclic time has its parallel in the arc of the south-light gallery, whose plane geometry corresponds roughly to the arc of the sun at 48° north latitude; and fragmented or gnostic time is reflected in the east-west skylights of the studios loft.

- BAM originated as an exterior experience in the street fair. In this spirit, outdoor terraces extend the museum's top level. With sunlight and views, these terraces accommodate outdoor classes as well as exhibitions and events on summer evenings. The twilight sky will be particularly inspiring from these spaces. The open attitude of tripleness is realized in a semipermanent exhibit program for each of the terraces:

"Right-Hand Rule" Terrace: The properties of movement of a negatively charged particle (electron) in a magnetic field are characterized by the "right-hand rule." The symbol in three fingers (digits) connects BAM's handcrafted past to its digital future.

Terrace of Planetary Motion: Beginning with Kepler's three laws of planetary motion, this terrace exhibits recent cosmological discoveries via the Hubbell telescope and electronic digital telescopes. The Hubbell images are projected on the inflected street-facing façade.

Court of Light: The debate in physics concerning whether light is a wave or a particle is finally opened: light is both a wave and a particle, depending on one's perspective. Here sunlight generates various unpredictable light phenomena.

Chromatic Terrace: Light projection from blue, red-and green-white light is formed.

Court of Water: With eastern exposure, the reflected light from a two-inch-deep water court dapples the gallery ceilings. Raindrops provide reflective patterns on rainy days.

Terrace of Wind and Shadow: Light projected from special fixtures captures the drama of the wind in moving shadows cast on the wall.

- A stepped ramp up to the galleries pauses at a landing that also functions as a stage. Ascending to the next level, one arrives at the Explore Gallery, a double-height skylighted space with an adjacent artist-in-residence studio. Passing by the overlook to the Forum, the stepped ramp leads to the top-level main loft galleries and the Court of Light.

Steven Holl, Steven Holl Architects

West façade, front entrance

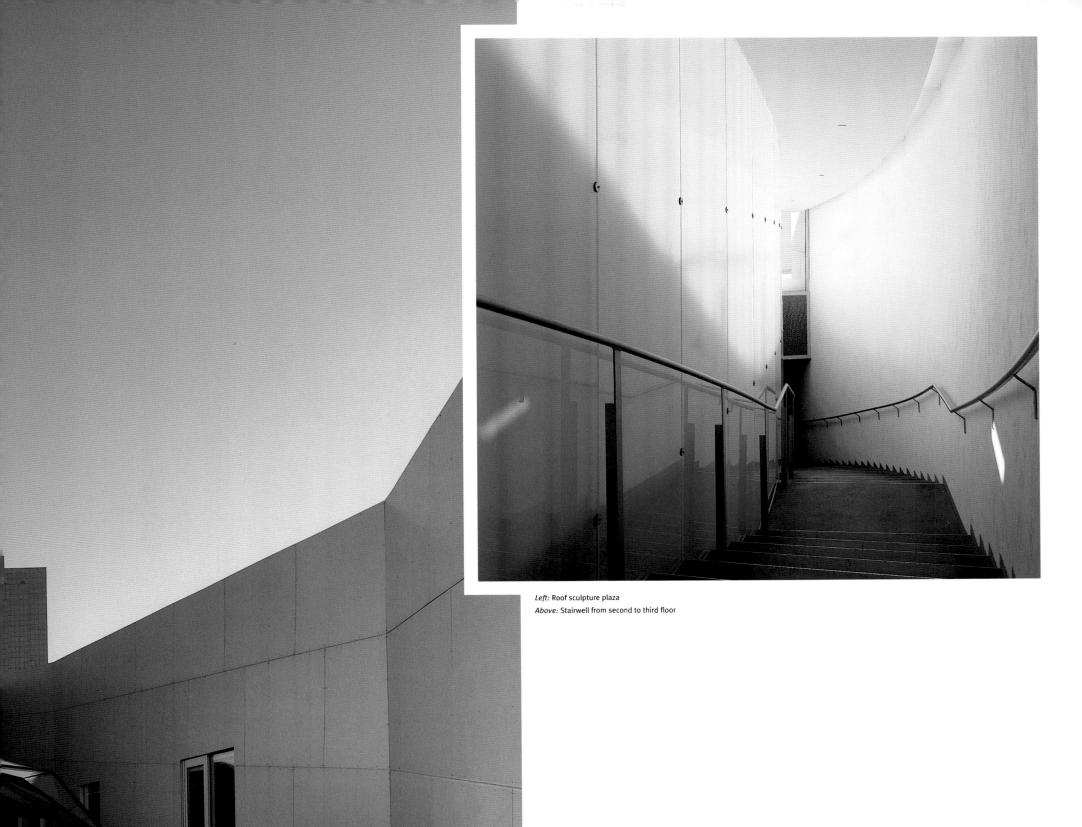

Left: Roof sculpture plaza
Above: Stairwell from second to third floor

AWARDS

• AIA Seattle 2000 Honor Award for Washington Architecture

CRITICS' COMMENTS

In an era during which it seems every major city in the world is commissioning expensive, landmark museums, and these, in turn, must mount a parade of blockbuster exhibits to pay the bills, the Bellevue Art Museum has created a model of economy and creativity. There is no permanent collection. More than half its space is devoted to classrooms and studios. And the building is made from nothing more lavish than concrete, steel, and marine-grade aluminum.
Randy Gragg, *The Sunday Oregonian*
(January 14, 2001)

The barn-red Bellevue Art Museum, designed by internationally renowned architect Steven Holl, breaks the mold of the downtown's architecture. More sculpture than building, the museum is being hailed as second in the region only to Frank Gehry's rainbow-hued "Experience Music Project."
Jeff Switzer, *Associated Press* (January 8, 2001)

Above: Upper floor, middle gallery
Right: Entrance-hall exhibition area
Opposite: Upper floor, north gallery

CONTEMPORARY ARTS
CENTER CINCINNATI, OH

Zaha Hadid

MUSEUM DIRECTOR'S STATEMENT

At the time of its founding in 1939, the Contemporary Arts Center was the first exhibition center for avant-garde art west of the Hudson River. At first, the CAC found temporary homes in a variety of city buildings, including the Cincinnati Art Museum. In 1970 the center built a structure for its own purposes, designed by Harry Weese, who had recently built the Metro subway system in Washington, D.C. It is difficult today to see past the unfortunate effects of wear and alterations on a space that must have been a stunning late-modern jewel box. The atrium and the grand stair (later replaced by escalators) were filled with light, and every surface was coated in white travertine marble or glistening metal or glass.

- The first half of the CAC's career focused on exhibiting the leading artists of the day, but the hallmark of the last thirty years has been its engagement with the Cincinnati community in ways that have expanded its mission beyond the aesthetic. In the civic arena, programs have influenced such areas as city planning and the creation of public monuments. More important, the introduction to the region of performance art, installation, and participatory projects has reshaped, to no small degree, the community's expectations regarding the visual art experience. The CAC's role today is as the cultural research and development center of its community, and the building that houses it has finally been created to suit that function.

- In 1997 the search process for the building's architect attracted more than three hundred architects from around the world. Of the three finalists—Zaha Hadid of London, Daniel Libeskind of Berlin, and Bernard Tschumi of New York—Ms. Hadid was eventually selected for a presentation that redefined exhibition flexibility. She proposed a "kit" of different-size galleries, independent volumes fitted together in a three-dimensional puzzle hung from a warped concrete plane. Although the 87,000-square-foot building as completed looks little like her first sketches, it has maintained the principle of function-driven forms that visibly define the look of the building exterior. Most important, Hadid's proposal and building embraced and extended what the CAC views as central to its relationship with its audience—"experiences outside boundaries."

- The new CAC building is an extraordinary work of art. Rather than a mere warehouse for objects or a workspace for museum professionals, it is a purposeful expression of ideas about art museums and their public, about urban environments and the people who inhabit them, and about constructed spaces and human interactions within them.

Charles Desmarais

ARCHITECT'S STATEMENT

The Contemporary Arts Center is a forum for the exchange of ideas and a gathering place for people of all cultures and ages. The museum is not defined by a collection and a set approach to art but is a changeable site that is open and receptive to the creative diversity of artists from around the globe. The architecture of the new building redefines the boundaries between art and life in various ways. In fact, the building itself is as original and enigmatic as a piece of abstract or conceptual art and, like a work of art, has its own strong formal logic, which informs the spatial logic of a piece of urban life.

- Like a socializing force, the building engages the community by attempting to broaden the audience for contemporary art. In addition, the center is an important civic space—like a public living room—inserted in the heart of downtown. The openness of the ground level and the penetration of light into various parts of the building make the passerby aware that there is something exciting going on inside. The ground-floor surface bends upward at the back of the building to create a strong continuity with the vertical circulation space that cuts through the building. This surface is the "urban carpet" that articulates the public accessibility of the building.

- With a system of ramps prominently positioned throughout the building, visitors can see each other moving through the space and interacting with the art. In this way, the architecture helps make the viewing of art a collective experience. The stair connects the ground level (the lobby) to the top level (the UnMuseum), easing movement from one part of the space to another.

- The fundamental concept is a jigsaw puzzle of diverse exhibition spaces—long, short, broad, or tall spaces, each with different lighting conditions. This concept is expressed in the exterior configuration, so that from the outside, you can read the volumes of the building. Inside, each volume is defined by material changes in the ceilings and the floors, so the viewer is constantly aware that the next level will be slightly different. We sought to create as many spaces as possible to allow the greatest possible variety and to support the presentation of two or three shows at the same time. Collectively, the space gives a clearly recognizable identity to the center, ensuring that the experience of viewing art here will be unlike that of any other venue.

Zaha Hadid, Zaha Hadid Architects

Detail of south façade

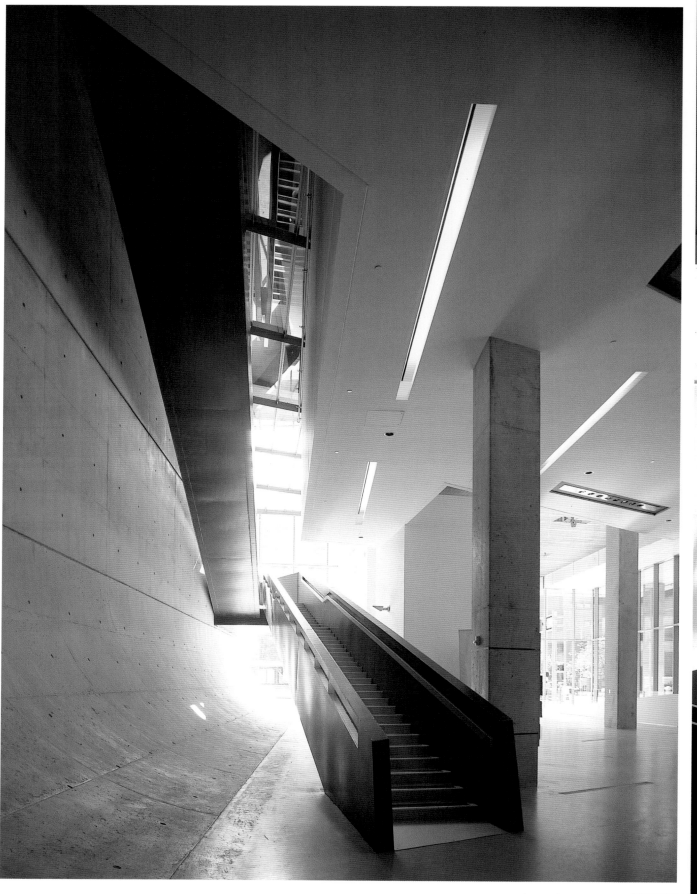

Above: North side of main lobby
Right: Upper multi-floor gallery

CRITICS' COMMENTS

Architectural and urban history were made here recently with the opening of Zaha Hadid's first American building, the Lois & Richard Rosenthal Center for Contemporary Art. It is an amazing building, a work of international stature that confidently meets the high expectations aroused by this prodigiously gifted architect for nearly two decades. Might as well blurt it out: the Rosenthal Center is the most important American building to be completed since the end of the cold war.
Herbert Muschamp, *New York Times* (June 8, 2003)

Architecture offers few really breakthrough moments but this may be one of them.... Occupying a tiny site on the busiest corner in the city, the new building is not so much a wake-up call to the city as a trumpet blast designed to be heard by the entire nation.
Mark Irving, *Financial Times* (June 30, 2003)

The Contemporary Arts Center ought to stifle doubts about Zaha Hadid's work being either unbuildable or unworkable. This has been built, and it works.... You do not have to redefine the idea of what a building is, or of what space is, to understand this building, but your ideas will be stretched.
Paul Goldberger, *The New Yorker* (June 2, 2003)

Opposite: Detail of east façade
Left: View of southeast corner
Above: Lighted stair handrail leading to second level

CONTEMPORARY ARTS MUSEUM HOUSTON HOUSTON, TX

Gunnar Birkerts

MUSEUM DIRECTOR'S STATEMENT

The Contemporary Arts Museum Houston (CAMH) was founded in 1948 to bring to Texas the most exciting and advanced contemporary art and to help audiences understand this new work. The mission of the museum has remained the same over the ensuing 50+ years: to present the art of our time. From its earliest years, the museum resolved that its focus would remain on exhibitions rather than collections, and by the late 1950s, it was determinedly a noncollecting museum. By the mid-1960s, however, the museum needed a new facility to accommodate the increasingly ambitious scale and experimental nature of the work being produced by artists of the period. The new building, with 17,000 square feet, would both accommodate and reflect the international art world's focus on new forms and new ideas in art. At the same time, it would maintain the innovative and contemporary spirit of the museum's first home—a small, decidedly modernist space-frame. The museum's board of trustees hired the young experimental architect Gunnar Birkerts to design the new building.

- When the warehouselike laboratory space for art opened in 1972 with a controversial exhibition of work in new mediums, it utterly confounded the public and even infuriated some of the museum's supporters. But Birkerts's building has served the museum well for more than thirty years, and Houstonians have come to see the building as a landmark. Other museum professionals often ask how we deal with such "difficult" space—those sharp corners of the parallelogram, the huge return-air pipes, the soaring walls capped by the uninterrupted space frame above, and the unfinished white pine floor. Our answer: We have found the glorious, columnless, 8,500-square-foot upper floor, the Brown Foundation Gallery, to be a gracious home for traditional easel-size painting, yet flexible enough to accommodate the most experimental technology.

- In 1997 the museum undertook a major renovation (led by Stern and Bucek Architects of Houston) to update its mechanical systems and to make the building more accommodating to visitors. Gunnar Birkerts's 1972 design was augmented by a more clearly marked entrance, a visitor information desk, space for education programs, and alterations on the exterior that invite passersby to sit by its fountain in the shade of its trees. The intimate Perspectives Gallery on the lower level was restored to an industrial-like space close to Birkerts's original design.

- Gunnar Birkerts's 1972 building has retained its edge and its symbolic meaning as a contemporary home for an institution presenting art that is not yet history. When I am asked about the striking, stainless-steel–clad building, the response is always "You're kidding. It was built in 1972? It looks like it was built yesterday."

Marti Mayo

ARCHITECT'S STATEMENT

Most of the buildings designed in Texas in the 1960s were by Texans, so I was very pleased that our office was awarded the commission for the Contemporary Arts Museum Houston. Although small in size, the museum was an important institution, the only museum in the city of Houston to serve as a bridge between contemporary art and the public. The site was on the southeastern edge of residential development, and on the opposite side of the street was the formidable Museum of Fine Arts addition by Mies van der Rohe.

- The parallelogram form of the CAMH developed in deference to interior and exterior considerations. The angled wall planes on the exterior reflect and deflect traffic, recognizing the changing street grid of Houston, which at the point pivots on the Museum of Fine Arts. Visual and spiritual contact with the Museum of Fine Arts was established by gently turning the broad side of the CAMH toward it and by creating an open, triangular forecourt. The angled building walls serve as a funnel from the residential area into the commercial area and vice versa.

- Caught between the two scales—the residential and the commercial—the building aimed to be a scaleless image that would present itself as a huge minimalist sculpture. The building avoids any reference to known building elements like windows or doors. The access is through a narrow aperture: A wide ramp leads the visitor to the building entrance, where one penetrates the building skin through a tall, slender slit and enters a transitional "space within a space." There the vertical dimension is transformed into a long horizontal panoramic opening, which looks into the exhibition space.

- The reflective, stainless-steel exterior skin encloses a workshoplike high space, which runs uninterruptedly and is spanned by a space-frame structure. This structural concept permits total flexibility in the arrangement of exhibits and lighting. The parallelogram provides an extended diagonal dimension to accommodate large-scale projects and adds an extended horizontal dimension. Additional spaces are located below the main exhibition level, accessible by a large, open stairway, and an additional gallery, education preparation spaces, a room for meetings and education activities, and the Museum Shop are now located on this level. The public areas on this level receive controlled daylight through clerestory windows.

Gunnar Birkerts, Gunnar Birkerts Architects

South side and front entrance

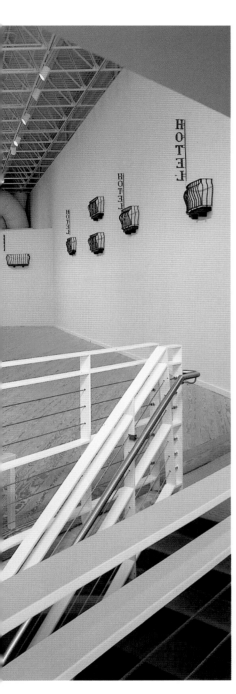

Opposite: Northwest side and pyramid/palm sculpture
Above left: Galleries from front entrance
Above right: Middle gallery looking toward entrance

CRITICS' COMMENTS

What Birkerts has done is to create a powerful shape (parallelo-gram)—not a monument—within which the ongoing art forms may recognize some sort of launch pad. There is dynamism in the compression of space within the tilted square, and Gunnar Birkerts brilliantly used his limited footage and budget to create a spatial ideal so simple it seems obvious. Yet simple forms are usually refinements of more elaborate, less acute ideas. This one seems a strikingly modest but elegant, proud but undemonstrative space just waiting to make its statement.
Ann Holmes, *Houston Chronicle* (April 1, 1978)

The architect has created, quite intentionally, what he calls a "minimal metal-block sculpture." The vertical strips of stainless steel covering the exterior are so reflective, and the points where the walls converge elude the eye's grasp so effectively, that in the hot Texas sun the Contemporary Arts Museum performs a "disappearing act" not unlike Robert Morris's mirror cubes or David von Schlegell's pointed tangents. It seems altogether appropriate for a museum that does not want to be a museum except in the most freewheeling way. Gunnar Birkerts has provided [director] "Lefty" Adler with an enclosure for a twenty-four-foot-high interior space, perched on a sunken concrete base containing offices, workshops, meeting rooms, and service areas with an overall floor space slightly larger than that of the galleries.
Jan van der Marck, *Art in America* (September 1972)

Left: Northwest-corner gallery
Above: Northeast corner as design element for artistic installation

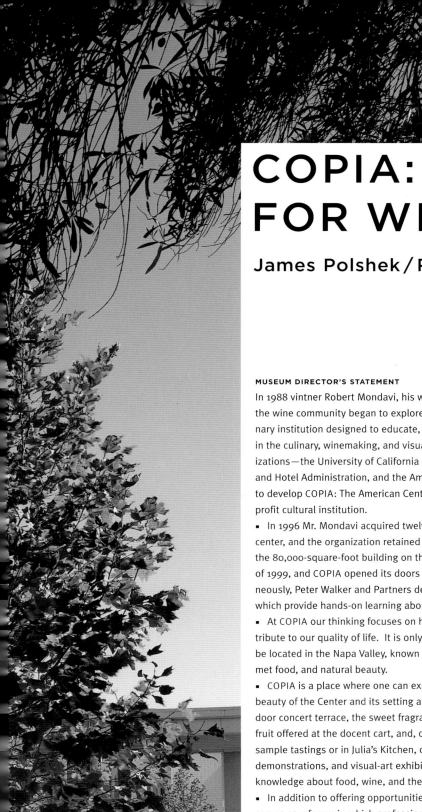

COPIA: THE AMERICAN CENTER FOR WINE, FOOD & THE ARTS NAPA, CA

James Polshek / Richard Olcott

MUSEUM DIRECTOR'S STATEMENT

In 1988 vintner Robert Mondavi, his wife, Magrit Biever Mondavi, and other leaders in the wine community began to explore the idea of establishing a unique cross-discipli- nary institution designed to educate, promote, and celebrate American achievements in the culinary, winemaking, and visual arts. As the project evolved, key partner organ- izations—the University of California at Davis, the Cornell University of Restaurant and Hotel Administration, and the American Institute of Wine & Food—joined forces to develop COPIA: The American Center for Wine, Food & the Arts into a major not-for- profit cultural institution.

- In 1996 Mr. Mondavi acquired twelve acres of land in the Napa Valley for the new center, and the organization retained Polshek Partnership Architects. Construction of the 80,000-square-foot building on the banks of the Napa River began in the summer of 1999, and COPIA opened its doors to the public on November 18, 2001. Simulta- neously, Peter Walker and Partners designed landscaped edible organic gardens, which provide hands-on learning about soils, farming, and viticulture.

- At COPIA our thinking focuses on how wine and food influence our culture and con- tribute to our quality of life. It is only natural for an organization with this charter to be located in the Napa Valley, known throughout the world for its premium wine, gour- met food, and natural beauty.

- COPIA is a place where one can experience all five senses—through the physical beauty of the Center and its setting along the river, the sound of live music in our out- door concert terrace, the sweet fragrances of the garden, the texture of the seasonal fruit offered at the docent cart, and, of course, the taste of food and wines at various sample tastings or in Julia's Kitchen, our premier dining room. Our programs, culinary demonstrations, and visual-art exhibitions are accessible to people with all levels of knowledge about food, wine, and the arts, from the novice to the connoisseur.

- In addition to offering opportunities for everyday discovery and adventure, COPIA serves as a forum in which professionals and the public can advance their level of understanding and contribute to our understanding of important biological and sociological issues related to world food supply, genetically altered and irradiated agriculture, dietary imbalances and insufficiencies, and other globally critical subjects. COPIA also contributes to the legacies of the culinary, oenological, agricultural, visual, and performing arts, as experts in these fields share their wisdom with a variety of audiences.

Peggy A. Loar

ARCHITECTS' STATEMENT

This new stone, polished concrete, metal, and glass building provides a setting in which COPIA can fully realize its mission to explore and reveal the interrelationships of wine and food with the arts, through innovative programming, interactive experiences, exhibitions, and scholarship.

- The COPIA building includes 13,000 square feet of gallery space for long-term and changing exhibitions of art, history, and science; a 280-seat theater for films and lec- tures; a rare-books library; classrooms with audio visual capabilities; an 80-seat demonstration kitchen forum; a gourmet dining room named for honorary trustee Julia Child, which also features a dramatic open finishing kitchen; a tasting area offering an expansive selection of wines from across the United States; an outdoor amphitheater for concerts and performances; a café and gift shop; and three and a half acres of organic gardens.

- Polshek Partnership Architects' design for COPIA combines natural and manmade materials with specific references to the industrial and agricultural architecture of the Napa Valley in which it is located. The gardens, designed by Peter Walker, William Johnson & Partners of Berkeley, California, complement the Napa landscape and are indivisible from the architecture of the new building.

- Villandry in France's Loire Valley provided inspiration for COPIA's design; specifically, its water features and stone château inform the Modernist composition of the center's architecture and gardens. The approach to COPIA is along a tree-lined allée flanked by a canal of moving water. This axis intersects a 600-foot-long fieldstone wall, which forms the entry threshold to the principal public spaces of the building and is emblem- atic of the historic connection of the center to the agricultural and viticultural products that it celebrates.

- Inside the building, an inviting glass-fronted atrium lobby provides dramatic views of the river. Visitors then move into a two-story light-filled gallery, where a crescent- shaped steel framework embraces an outdoor dining area and a performing-arts amphitheater. The delicate exposed steel structure, sheathed in glass, represents the future, just as the solidity of the great stone wall alludes to the past. Principal gallery spaces are arranged on the upper level, with the serpentine roof of the permanent exhibition hall responding to the rolling hills to the east.

James Polshek / Richard Olcott, Design Partners, Polshek Partnership Architects

CRITICS' COMMENTS

The good life is a religion in Northern California. Now, it finally has a temple.... Mr. Polshek's building is a pull-out-the-stops architectural statement, with a fieldstone wall recalling old-school Napa wineries and an abstract undulating metal roof. Mr. Polshek, who also designed the Rose Center for Earth and Space in Manhattan, calls his contemporary form, which echoes a bend in the river, "a great croissant."
Patricia Leigh Brown, *New York Times* (December 12, 2001)

The ground level of the 355-foot-long structure is clad in field-stone, the second in sage-tinted steel panels. Corrugated tin wraps around the east and west edges. Everything is straight-forward except the roof, which undulates in a series of 4-foot waves that hint of nearby hillsides. That gesture is Polshek's one literal homage to the setting.
John King, *San Francisco Chronicle* (November 13, 2001)

Page 48 above: Overview of second floor
Page 48 below: North side of main lobby, with stair and elevator access
Pages 48–49: Main entrance, with reflecting pool walkway

Left: Permanent-exhibition galleries
Above: Entry exhibition, with upper-gallery stairwell

CORNING MUSEUM OF GLASS

CORNING, NY

Wallace Harrison, Gunnar Birkerts, Henry Smith-Miller

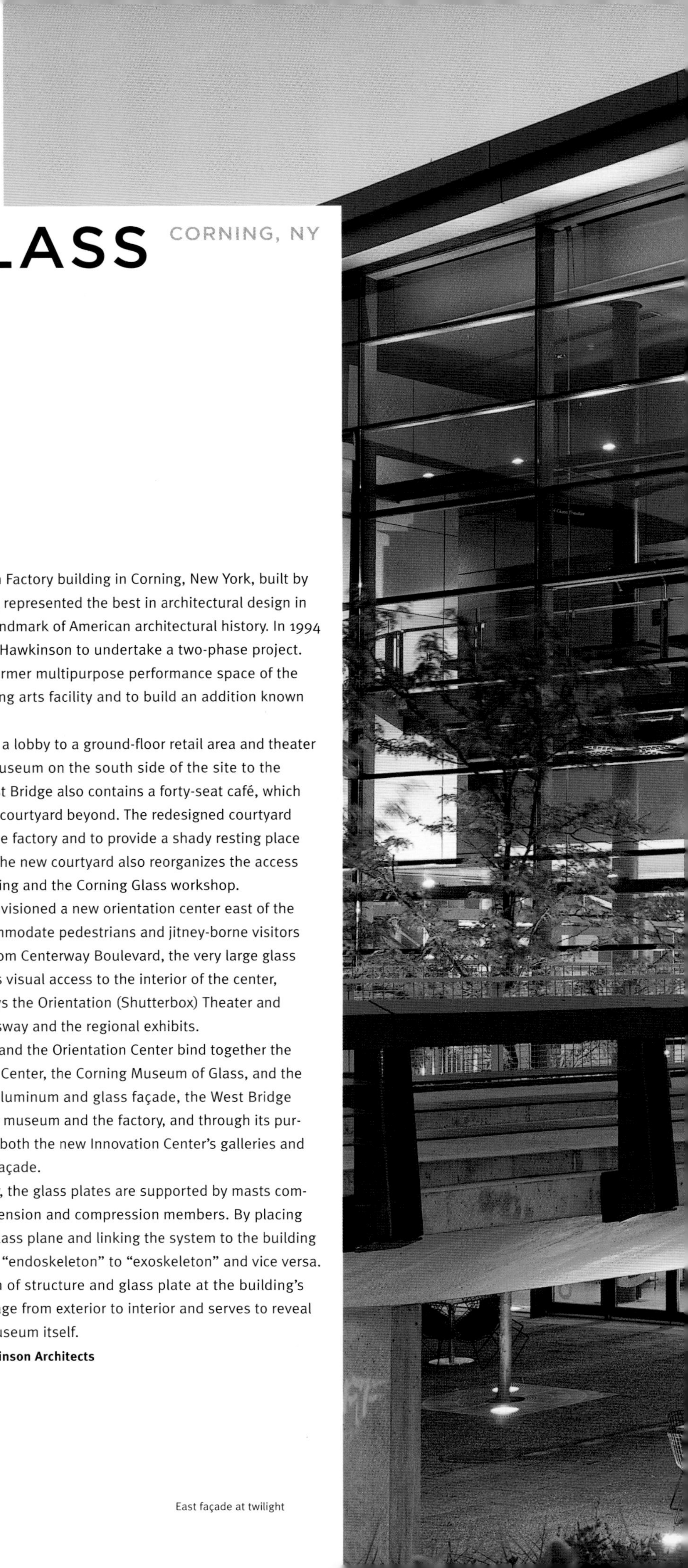

MUSEUM DIRECTOR'S STATEMENT

The Corning Museum of Glass, a nonprofit institution, was founded in 1950 by Corning Glass Works (now Corning Incorporated). When the museum opened a year later, it was part of the Corning Glass Center, a gift to the nation that celebrated the company's centennial. The other components were the Steuben glass factory (then and now a division of Corning Incorporated) and the Glass Center proper, a for-profit entity that included retail and other facilities, and a Hall of Science and Industry with exhibits explaining the properties of glass and showcasing Corning products.

▪ The museum outgrew its original home, and in 1982 it moved to an adjoining structure designed for the purpose by Gunnar Birkerts. In 1998 the museum underwent a transformation when the Glass Center (but not Steuben) was brought under its non-profit umbrella. This legal change coincided with, and was in part occasioned by, a major program of renovation and expansion of the entire facility.

▪ Despite these developments, the purpose of the museum is still the same as it was in 1951,—to build and preserve the world's foremost glass collection and the library of record for the art and history of glass. We engage and inspire our visitors by displaying the best of the collection in a permanent exhibition and by arranging temporary exhibitions that focus on particular aspects of the art and history of glass. We also provide opportunities to watch and participate in glassmaking. At the same time, we strive to be an international leader in the pursuit and dissemination of knowledge about the art, history, and science of glass. In a nutshell, we aim to excel, and in order to do this we work hard to ensure that we have an outstanding facility and we maintain it in an outstanding manner.

▪ Smith-Miller + Hawkinson earned their spurs at the museum by refurbishing part of the original building as the venue for a 1994 exhibition of work by the Czech glass artists Libensky and Brychtová, and this space still serves very effectively as a gallery for contemporary sculpture. Smith-Miller + Hawkinson went on to design or renovate the new entrance to the museum, the Innovation Center (which replaced the old Hall of Science and Industry), the auditorium, and the West Bridge (an all-important thread that stitches together the various parts of the architectural patchwork). Their creations are elegant, respectful of the earlier buildings, and full of glass.

David Whitehouse

ARCHITECT'S STATEMENT

The Corning Glass Center and Steuben Factory building in Corning, New York, built by the architect Wallace Harrison in 1951, represented the best in architectural design in their time and remains to this day a landmark of American architectural history. In 1994 Corning commissioned Smith-Miller + Hawkinson to undertake a two-phase project. The first phase was to renovate the former multipurpose performance space of the Glass Center into a 770-seat performing arts facility and to build an addition known as the West Bridge.

▪ The West Bridge addition serves as a lobby to a ground-floor retail area and theater operations and connects the Glass Museum on the south side of the site to the Steuben Factory to the north. The West Bridge also contains a forty-seat café, which opens onto the newly renovated west courtyard beyond. The redesigned courtyard now serves to link the museum and the factory and to provide a shady resting place for an extension of the café amenity. The new courtyard also reorganizes the access and relationship to the executive parking and the Corning Glass workshop.

▪ This second phase of the project envisioned a new orientation center east of the present Glass Center in order to accommodate pedestrians and jitney-borne visitors who arrive on the upper level. Seen from Centerway Boulevard, the very large glass façade of the Orientation Center offers visual access to the interior of the center, invites the visitor to enter, and displays the Orientation (Shutterbox) Theater and the ramp to the beginning of the Glassway and the regional exhibits.

▪ Together, the West Bridge addition and the Orientation Center bind together the currently disparate forms of the Glass Center, the Corning Museum of Glass, and the Steuben Factory. With its horizontal aluminum and glass façade, the West Bridge addition links the diverse forms of the museum and the factory, and through its purposely transparent façade, it displays both the new Innovation Center's galleries and the former Glass Center's glass brick façade.

▪ To maintain maximum transparency, the glass plates are supported by masts comprising high-strength stainless-steel tension and compression members. By placing the mast interior and exterior to the glass plane and linking the system to the building structure, the window wall shifts from "endoskeleton" to "exoskeleton" and vice versa. The deliberately didactic combination of structure and glass plate at the building's entrance celebrates the visitor's passage from exterior to interior and serves to reveal the exploratory nature of the Glass Museum itself.

Henry Smith-Miller, Smith-Miller + Hawkinson Architects

East façade at twilight

Opposite left: Southwest section of the Birkerts building
Opposite below: Steuben Glass studio building
Above: Southeast corner of the Birkerts building

Above: Bridge to southeast gallery
Right: Gallery in the Birkerts building
Opposite: Gallery in the Birkerts building

yourself – Visit the Walk-in Workshop

CRITIC'S COMMENT

It is easy to laugh at the utopian fervor with which early 20th-century architects championed the use of glass. "The face of the earth would be much altered if brick architecture were ousted everywhere by glass architecture," wrote the poet Paul Scheerbart, a cheerleader for the so-called Glass Chain, a group of Expressionist architects whose belief in glass was virtually religious.... But as Smith Miller and Hawkinson's design makes clear, they have been among its most dedicated custodians throughout this century. There is a Glass Chain that runs from Joseph Paxton to Taut to Mies van der Rohe to Harrison to Nouvel to David Chipperfield to Toyo Ito and beyond. No other architects of this century have displayed more vibrantly such traditional qualities as lucidity, harmony, wholeness, scale, procession, and the creativity necessary to renew their continuing from one generation to the next.
Herbert Muschamp, *New York Times* (June 14, 1998)

Opposite above: Contemporary glass gallery
Opposite below: Bracing for the window wall becomes sculptural at the entrance
Center: Theater of Steuben glass-blowing demonstration with studio in background
Above: East gallery of glass usage, development, and production

CRANBROOK ART MUSEUM BLOOMFIELD HILLS, MI

Eliel Saarinen, Rafael Moneo

MUSEUM DIRECTOR'S STATEMENT

Cranbrook Art Museum is Michigan's largest museum devoted exclusively to twentieth- and twenty-first-century art, a dynamic forum for contemporary art, architecture, and design. The museum, which is an integral part of Cranbrook Academy of Art, is located at the heart of the Cranbrook Educational Community's architecturally renowned campus. It serves diverse audiences throughout metropolitan Detroit, including the students and artists of Cranbrook. Cranbrook Art Museum was founded in 1927 and first opened to the public in 1930. The original collection was an eclectic mixture of art and artifacts spanning the centuries, selected and purchased by Cranbrook's founder, George G. Booth, a newspaper publisher and a leading proponent of the American Arts and Crafts Movement.

▪ In 1942 the present Cranbrook Art Museum and Cranbrook Academy of Art Library building opened. Distinguished by its grand peristyle, which links the library and museum both conceptually and physically, the museum and library complex was the last building designed at Cranbrook by the Finnish-American architect Eliel Saarinen. Although the collection at this time remained encyclopedic in scope, new acquisitions and temporary exhibitions increasingly emphasized contemporary art. As the century progressed, the collection continued to grow, with a special emphasis on the work of Cranbrook Academy of Art's most distinguished faculty and alumni.

▪ Today the Cranbrook collection focuses almost exclusively on modern and contemporary art—from the time of Cranbrook's founding in 1904 during the Arts and Crafts Movement to the present. Like the Academy, a graduate program with ten diverse fields of study, the museum's collection incorporates the fields of art, architecture, and design. Included in the collection is the Art Deco masterwork Saarinen House, Eliel Saarinen's home and garden on the Academy's campus. Restored and operated by the art museum as a historic-house museum, Saarinen House is a total work of art featuring Eliel's architectural detailing and furniture and the textiles of his wife, Loja Saarinen.

▪ In 2002 Cranbrook Academy of Art completed the New Studios Building. Designed by Rafael Moneo and housing the departments of ceramics, fiber, and metalsmithing, the building is connected to the Saarinen-designed museum with a shared gallery and lobby spaces. The next phase of this project is an addition to the museum, including a 6,000-square-foot gallery for temporary exhibitions, collections storage, shipping and receiving spaces, and other public amenities.

Gregory Wittkopp

ARCHITECT'S STATEMENT

In 1948, when Eliel Saarinen was alive, and immediately following Albert Christ-Janer's tenure as the director of Cranbrook Academy of Art Museum (its name at that time), Christ-Janer wrote Eliel Saarinen: Finnish-American Architect and Educator *(Chicago: University of Chicago Press, 1948), from which the following statement has been excerpted.*

Eliel Saarinen began work on the design for the museum and library of the Cranbrook Academy of Art in 1940.... In preparation for the design of this exhibition hall and library, the designer made a thorough study of museums by traveling in this country and in Europe to see the art galleries that had been acclaimed for possessing certain excellent features. But the most valuable information he received came from the industrial concerns, which had experimented in lighting, ventilation, and air conditioning. When he had gathered a fund of material, he began to work on his plan for the Cranbrook Museum.

▪ The function of the building is to display a collection of art objects against a quiet background and, in the library, to provide the student with a pleasant, well-lighted environment in which he may study. That it fulfills its function can be ascertained by even a casual glance at the building. Architects from all over the world have studied it. The exterior, though plain to the point of austerity, is a study in details of form, color, and texture. The combination of Mankato stone and brick shows the designer's ability to work with these mediums, with which he had thoroughly familiarized himself. Since 1931 [for Kingswood School Cranbrook] he had employed the warm, delicately textured stone with the Wyandotte brick. Used at focal points and at the base level of the structure, the stone is sparingly ornamented with a motif, which, though highly personal, is universal in its quality as a geometric symbol.

▪ The relationship between the museum and library building and the older structures on the campus is sympathetic; harmony is produced by a coordination of proportions and the use of similar materials. When Joseph Hudnut was asked by the building committee of a large college whether it would be wise to continue in the established Gothic style, he answered: "You need not build in a similar style to attain unity on this campus. A good design in proper scale will bring the harmony you desire." Cranbrook Academy of Art is an excellent illustration of Hudnut's observation. Scale unifies those buildings; the result sets an example for the planning committees of the educational institutions who wish to employ a contemporary method of construction, incorporating the best of today's design and materials.

North façade from entrance stairs

CRITIC'S COMMENT

The new building suggests formality, yet it is subtly composed as a part of an informal scheme. Its rather severe quasi-classical lines make it an appropriate background against which to display a number of strong and vital sculptures, principally the work of the great sculptor Carl Milles, who has been in residence at Cranbrook since 1931.

Saarinen's fine sense of space and form and of the relationship of building masses to the areas in which they are set is felt by the visitor.... The building is thoroughly functional, yet there is more to it than mere functionalism. It has a quality of external monumentality achieved principally by simple basic architectural means, disturbed only occasionally by bits of playful decoration.

New Pencil Points
(December 1943), p. 37

Opposite: South side of museum from sculpture pool
Above: Main gallery viewed from entrance lobby

Page 64: Main entrance
Page 65: Detail of main-entrance door

DALLAS MUSEUM OF ART DALLAS, TX

Edward Larrabee Barnes, Richard Gluckman

MUSEUM DIRECTOR'S STATEMENT

In 1903 a group of artists and friends of art founded the Dallas Art Association, the predecessor of the Dallas Museum of Art, with one of its purposes being to form a public art collection. Today, one hundred years later, its special areas of strength— the art of the ancient Americas, Africa, and Indonesia—are international in quality and rivaled by few museums in the country for their significance. The museum also has, among other fine artistic assets, impressive collections of South Asian art; of textiles, design, and decorative arts; of European and American paintings and sculpture, and of American and international modern and contemporary art.

- In 1936 the museum opened its first permanent home, an Art-Deco–style building erected in Fair Park. In 1963 the museum merged with the Dallas Museum for Contemporary Arts to create a combined institution, one that would accommodate the dynamic tension of two agendas. By the 1970s, because of significant collection growth and the need to advance the museum's program beyond that of a regional institution, the museum moved, under the directorial leadership of Harry S. Parker III, to a site in the newly conceived Dallas Arts District downtown. What was called for was a "full-service" museum facility that would meet the requirements of an encyclopedic museum and also provide for the needs of an active contemporary art program. Edward Larrabee Barnes was chosen as architect. His work on the Walker Art Center in Minneapolis and the Sarah Scaife Gallery addition to the Carnegie Institute in Pittsburgh had earned him accolades in museum design. (He partnered on the project with landscape architect Daniel Kiley to create the exceptionally fine, attached sculpture garden.)

- Opening in 1984, the new 210,000-square-foot building was a handsome and institutionally transforming success. Yet certain limitations became evident almost immediately, specifically in the size of the special exhibition galleries and of public amenities, such as entertainment spaces, café, museum store, and parking. These were ameliorated in 1993 with the Hamon addition, also designed by Barnes, which made the museum a truly expansive and architecturally consistent facility without significant physical constraints on its programs and collections.

- In anticipation of the opening in 2003 of the nearby Nasher Sculpture Center designed by Renzo Piano, the museum asked Gluckman Mayner Architects to propose enhancements that would underline the pedestrian connections between the two arts organizations and begin to address long-standing concerns regarding access to, circulation through, and configuration of the permanent collections galleries.

Dr. John R. Lane

ARCHITECT'S STATEMENT

Gluckman Mayner Architects has been working recently with the Dallas Museum of Art to develop design modifications to the museum's Edward Larrabee Barnes building and its addition by Barnes Lee Partners. Prompting this work is the imminent opening of the Nasher Sculpture Center, designed by Renzo Piano, immediately opposite the museum on North Harwood Street.

- The modifications for the present project concern the ground-level path through the museum's concourse. This path brings the Nasher Sculpture Center visitors through the Flora Street Court, into the Flora Street entrance and barrel-vaulted exhibition space, and through the concourse leading north to the Hamon Court entrance. The museum's parking garage is accessible at this entrance.

- The primary objective of this project is to encourage and accommodate this mutually beneficial pedestrian traffic. The greatest change to be undertaken is the opening of the secluded Flora Court to Flora Street and the Nasher Sculpture Center's entrance on North Harwood Street. Four masonry piers, scaled commensurately with the Barnes building and of matching limestone, are to be constructed as welcoming gateways to the museum. Each pier has large graphic panels reflecting the art treasures to be found within the impressive, protective, and opaque building that terminates Flora Street. Additionally, the panels are visible to traffic passing the museum on North Harwood Street, thereby heightening its presence in the Arts District, which is expanding rapidly to include more cultural institutions.

- Within the Flora Street Court, the existing concrete paving is to be restored to the cobblestones of its original design, though with a smoother walking surface. The court's perimeter illumination is to be increased significantly, amplifying its nighttime presence.

- The concourse itself, with the recent introduction of an entry fee, must accommodate simple ticketing counters, one at each end. The counter at the Flora Street entrance is removable so that the sweep from the court into the great barrel vault can at times remain unobstructed. The concourse is the circulatory backbone of the museum and will be reinforced in this capacity by the provision of an elevator lobby and a second elevator immediately accessible and directly visible from the Hamon Court ticketing counter.

- Pentagram's New York office has prepared graphic systems for the museum, both external and internal, to address circulation, identity, and information requirements arising from the Nasher Collection's arrival in the Arts District.

Richard Gluckman, Gluckman Mayner Architects

Ross Avenue entrance

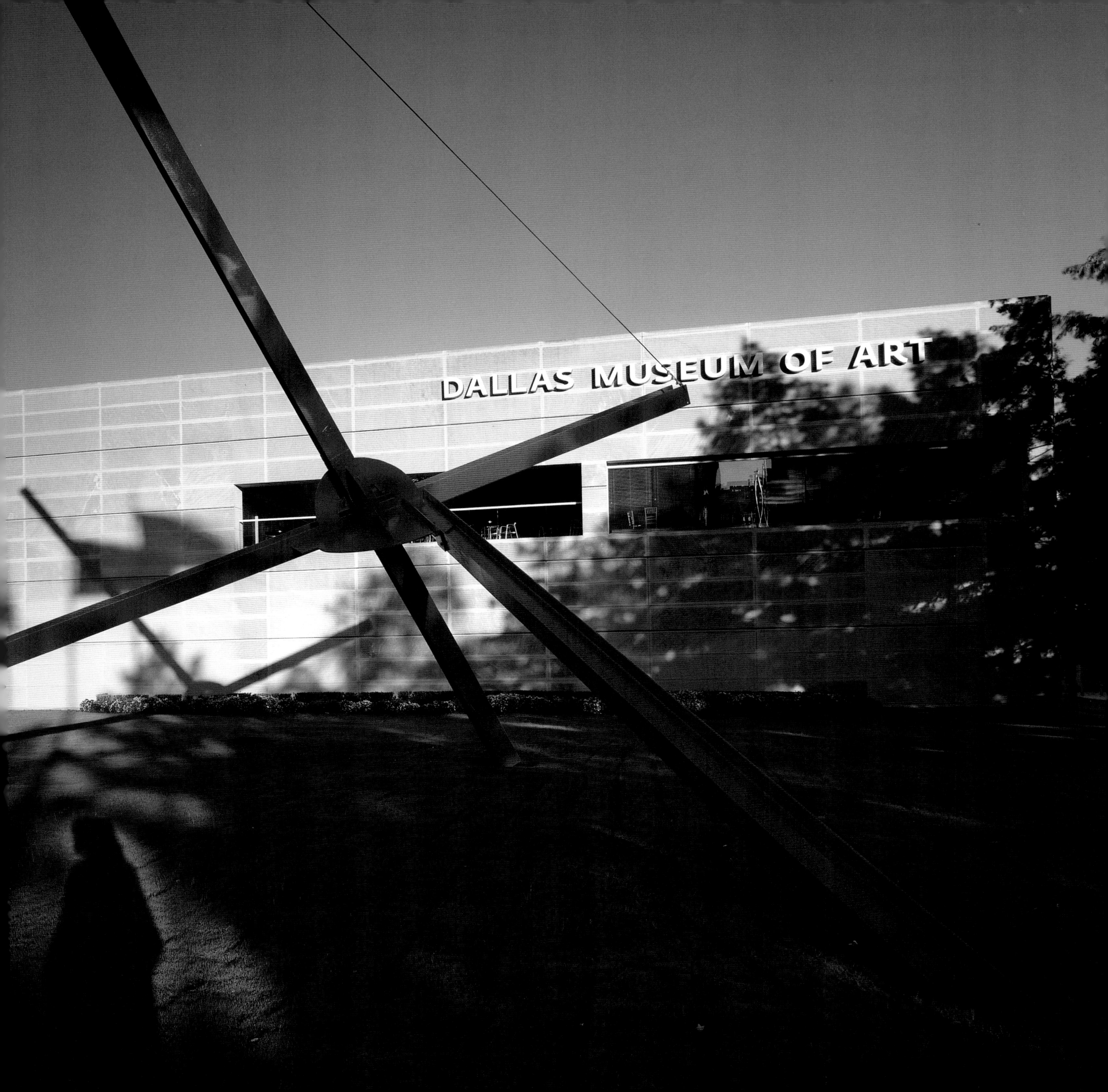
DALLAS MUSEUM OF ART

Opposite: Public entrance to sculpture garden
Above: Native North American Gallery
Left: Flora Street entrance

CRITIC'S COMMENT
From the moment Barnes started working on the
design in the fall of 1977, he envisioned the proposed museum as a catalyst and cornerstone of a
new cultural district to enrich and enliven downtown
Dallas. He helped select the site, . . . and he placed
the front entrance of his building at the end of Flora
Street. . . . As a result of Barnes's vision, Dallas has
discovered and is preserving a number of interesting
old buildings on Flora and decided to turn the street
into a grand boulevard that will be flanked by a
proposed concert hall, already designed by architect
I. M. Pei. . . . Covering nearly nine acres at the foot of
Dallas's downtown skyscrapers, the museum consists of a low composition of geometric forms, domi-
nated by an imposing 40-foot-high barrel vault. The
entire building is of limestone, cut in huge blocks
and coursed with deep V cuts. It does not look monumental, let alone massive, but it is self-assured and
virtually throbs with energy. The stoic exterior conveys a sense of the various spaces inside. They
include landscaped courtyards and an enchanting
1.2-acre sculpture garden.
Wolfgang Von Eckardt, *Newsweek* (February 13, 1984)

Opposite: Atrium café and music venue
Left: Barrel-vault gallery

DES MOINES ART CENTER

Eliel Saarinen, I. M. Pei, Richard Meier

MUSEUM DIRECTOR'S STATEMENT

When the Des Moines Association of Fine Arts received an endowment to build a museum, they debated between erecting a traditional Grecian edifice or a Modernist structure. The Modernist won, beginning the architectural legacy of the Des Moines Art Center in 1948, thirty-two years after the association was established in 1916.

▪ The initial architectural choice also set the direction that the founders and their successors took in building an art collection of singular works that span the last two centuries and continue to look to the new.

▪ Within fifty years of the founders' decision to build, three of America's greatest architects created a complex of interlocking buildings around a central courtyard and reflecting pool. Their complex is set among the rolling hills of a city park that is reached off a tree-lined thoroughfare.

▪ Eliel Saarinen designed the first museum building as a low, landscape-hugging structure of Lannon stone. A spacious, high-ceilinged lobby and gallery walls were constructed of rift-grain oak. A clear glass paneled wall and door opens into the courtyard.

▪ Looking toward expansion two decades later, the museum board selected I. M. Pei, an architect in mid-career who had not yet built a museum. Pei paid tribute to Saarinen by designing a companion building of bush-hammered concrete that harmonizes with the rough texture of the original building.

▪ Pei's building is two stories tall, but its height can be seen only from the rear, where a clear glass wall overlooks a rose garden and a sculpture of Lannon stone by Andy Goldsworthy. Pei's main gallery is a huge, high-ceilinged room designed as a sculpture court. The ceiling is remarkable for giant butterfly windows that let in copious light and anticipates a similar use of daylight in Pei's later National Gallery of Art in Washington, D.C.

▪ As need for more space continued, the board once again decided to expand and turned to Richard Meier, who completed the complex in 1985 with a white-enameled steel and glass building. His three-story structure added a restaurant, which opens onto the courtyard. Inside the Meier building, glass stairways and a room-size elevator connect the three stories of galleries that house the most contemporary of the Art Center's works.

▪ Together, the Art Center's three buildings span a rich period of American architecture when traditional museum design was revolutionized. In the forefront of that revolution were the architects of the Des Moines Art Center, who created a singular testimony to museum architecture.

Susan Lubowsky Talbott

ARCHITECT'S STATEMENT

Eliel Saarinen designed the first building of the Des Moines Art Center in 1948. It consisted of a U-shape single-story gallery, plus a double-height gallery to the west, terminated by a two-story annex. In 1968 I. M. Pei added a block to the south facing a public park, thereby closing the original U-plan in order to create an internal sculpture court. The site for the second addition is primarily north of this two-stage complex, and since the Saarinen building is visible from the downtown approach, the problem was how to design an addition that would respect the generally horizontal profile of the center.

▪ The addition was designed as a series of separate volumes to accommodate the required expansion without producing a large mass. Thus, three new additions were located around the existing complex in such a way as to reinforce the formal order of the Saarinen scheme. A new courtyard pavilion strengthens the east–west entry axis of the existing museum, accommodates the restaurant and meeting room, and activates the previously underused court by opening it to the patio in warm weather.

▪ A glass-enclosed link running along the north–south axis connects to the new northern addition, which houses most of the additional gallery space. Volumetrically separate from the Saarinen building, this larger increment is vertically condensed and leaves the preferred view of the existing museum unobstructed. The largest of its three levels is located entirely below grade, but light slots admit natural light into the temporary exhibition gallery.

▪ The overall plan in this addition derives from a nine-square grid, in which the central square provides a four-column internal atrium, lit by clerestory windows and perimeter skylights. This cubic volume is sheathed in granite and covered by a flattened pyramid that serves as a foil to the butterfly-section roof employed by Pei. A third, smaller, addition, accommodating services and additional gallery space above, is attached to the west wing of the Saarinen building. In this way the Saarinen/Pei complex was discretely amplified by three separate additions of different sizes.

Richard Meier, Richard Meier & Partners, Architects

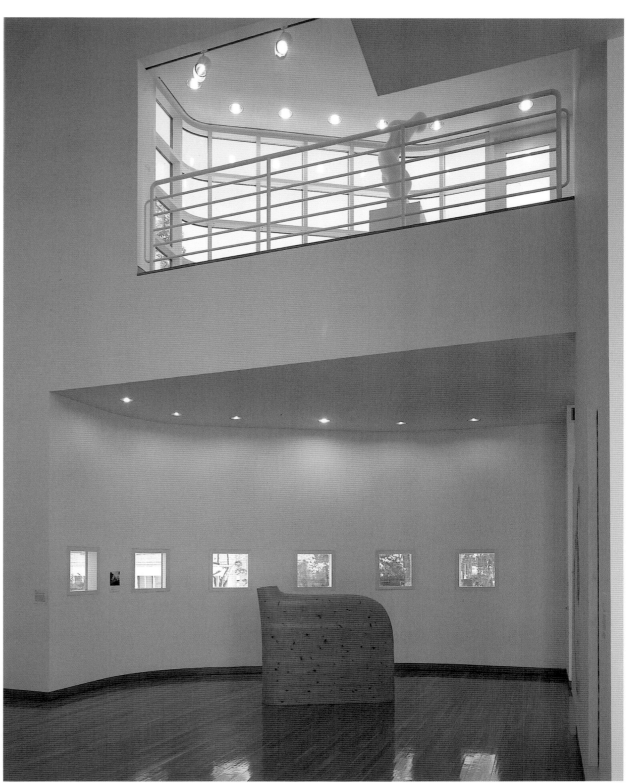

Opposite: Stair atrium of Meier addition
Above left: Corner pocket gallery in Meier addition
Above right: Northwest corner, two-level gallery

Above: Lower-level gallery of Pei building
Right: North side of Pei building
Far right: I. M. Pei building from central courtyard

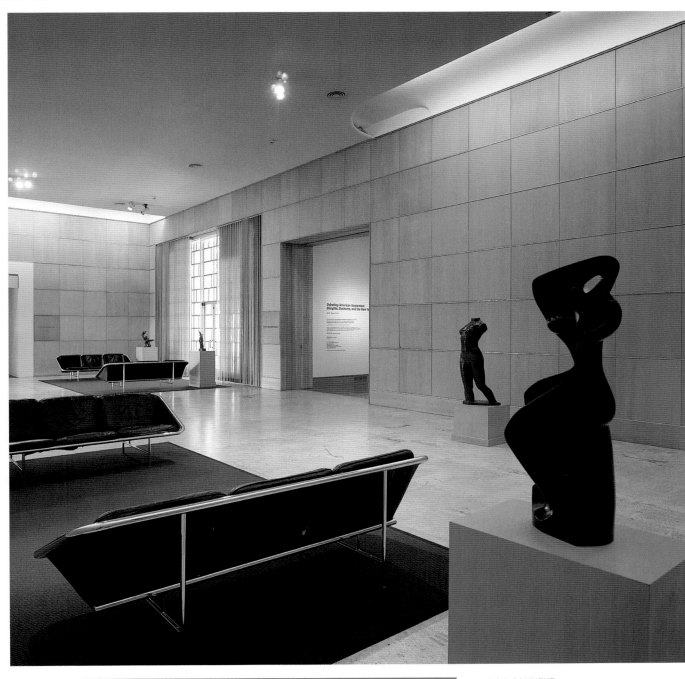

With the completion of Eliel Saarinen's design in 1948, the Des Moines Art Center established a significant Modernist alternative to the traditional architectural concept of the small American art museum. . . . Yet the very distinction of the center's architecture has made the art it is meant to serve all the more compelling: the nineteenth- and twentieth-century painting hanging in the amiable atmosphere of the Saarinen structure; the large scale of the sculpture—and the painting—that enjoy the expansive space of the Pei wing; the challenging variety of contemporary expression that fills all levels of the Meier. At the outset of its second half-century, Des Moines continues to occupy a singular space in any transcontinental museum tour.

Franz Schulze, "Architectural Trinity in Des Moines,"
The Des Moines Art Center: An Uncommon Vision
(Des Moines Art Center, 1998)

Far left: Saarinen-designed southeast corridor gallery
Above: Saarinen-designed entrance hall
Left: Original Saarinen front entrance

THE J. PAUL GETTY MUSEUM LOS ANGELES, CA

Richard Meier

MUSEUM DIRECTOR'S STATEMENT

J. Paul Getty, an oil tycoon of great wealth, established a museum in his Malibu home in 1953. It grew out of his private holdings, a distinguished collection of Greek and Roman antiquities and French seventeenth- and eighteenth-century decorative arts. In the early 1970s, Getty decided to re-create an ancient Roman villa, based on plans of the ancient Villa dei Papiri just outside of Herculaneum, as a separate museum building on the Malibu ranch property.

- After Getty's death in 1976, his bequest—the equivalent of $1.2 billion in Getty Oil stock—allowed the board to develop the museum's collection. It also enabled the dramatic expansion of the scope of the Getty Trust, which encompassed the museum, as well as new, separate programs for research, education, and conservation.

- Seeing that the museum would require more space and that the newer Getty programs, then scattered around Los Angeles in rented offices and warehouses, also needed permanent quarters, the board decided to build a new facility. They selected a 742-acre plot of land in the foothills of the Santa Monica Mountains, overlooking the ocean on one side and the city on the other. In October 1984, Richard Meier was selected as architect for what would be the largest single-phase construction project in the history of Los Angeles.

- The museum was only one part of the project, but it was the most complex. Even before an architect was named, John Walsh, who was then the director, developed a program for the new museum. It called for architecture of great distinction, where art would be shown to best advantage and visitors would feel welcome and inspired. The specifications focused on the needs of each collection. In the paintings galleries, for example, lively, natural light was essential. The idea of clustering galleries into different pavilions had particular appeal: visitors could choose their own path according to their interests or whimsy.

- Richard Meier conceived of a series of buildings—an entrance hall, and five pavilions—dispersed around a central courtyard. The galleries, as realized by Meier and his partner, Michael Palladino, are beautifully proportioned; their interiors, while decidedly modern, are as finely detailed as any great historical gallery. Skylights with an ingenious louver system fill the paintings galleries with a magical light. The transitions between pavilions and the central courtyard provide not only brilliantly framed vistas of the ocean, mountains, and city but also places for rest and conversation or contemplation.

Deborah Gribbon

ARCHITECT'S STATEMENT

The Getty Center occupies a unique, hilly site jutting southward from the Santa Monica Mountains in California. The program brings the different components of the Getty Trust into a coherent unity, while maintaining their individual identities.

- The layout establishes a dialogue between the angle of intersection and a number of curvilinear forms. These forms are largely derived from the contours of the site inflected by the freeway, the metropolitan grid, and the natural topography. The overall design relates to both the City of Los Angeles and the Santa Monica Mountains.

- The buildings, which cover almost 100,000 square feet of area, are organized along two ridges in the topography of the 742-acre parcel. An intersection of the twin axes corresponds to the inflection of the San Diego Freeway as it bends northward out of the Los Angeles street grid. An underground parking garage and a tram station establish the public entrance to the site.

- The museum lobby provides views through the courtyard to gallery structures arrayed in a continuous sequence. The smaller pavilion buildings, connected by gardens, break down the scale of the museum experience, allowing for pauses and encouraging interplay between the interior and exterior.

- A 450-seat auditorium and the Getty Trust offices terminate the east elevation. The building housing the Getty Conservation Institute and the Getty Grant Program takes advantage of the climate through the use of loggias, pergolas, and full-height glazing at the external perimeter. Along the more secluded western ridge, the Getty Research Institute completes the complex.

Richard Meier, Richard Meier & Partners, Architects

Central courtyard from exhibitions pavilion

CRITICS' COMMENTS

You enter through an immense, airy, cylindrical building, from which you get enticing glimpses of the courtyard and its Alhambra-like fountains. It is while moving around the courtyard and terraces of the museum that you experience most intensely the musical way that Meier plays variations on his favorite themes, working transparency against solidity, the diagonal against the curve, the hard against the soft, and so on. Here, too, you begin to notice the superb detailing both in design and craftsmanship—the three-inch-thick travertine panels, for example, separated by half-inch reveals rather than mortar joints. It is a system Meier perfected during his many years of working with metal-panel facades— the weather protection is applied behind the building's "skin."
Ben Forgey, *Washington Post* (December 14, 1997)

A few months ago, Mr. Meier invited a few people to join him at the Getty Center to watch the sunset. In the late afternoon, the place is a miracle. The great California light spills down on your body, into your eyes. It gets more and more golden, and by twilight you're having a pure Apollo moment. The rough surface of the travertine picks up and intensifies the light, until it seems that energy is turning into matter.
Herbert Muschamp, *New York Times*
(December 1, 1997)

THE SOLOMON R. GUGGENHEIM MUSEUM

Frank Lloyd Wright, Charles Gwathmey

MUSEUM DIRECTOR'S STATEMENT

In 1937 Solomon R. Guggenheim established a foundation empowered to operate a museum (or museums) that would exhibit to the public and preserve his inventive but narrowly focused holdings in non-objective painting. The foundation's first museum space was in a former automobile showroom in Manhattan on East Fifty-fourth Street. In 1943, to meet the demands of the flourishing Museum of Non-Objective Painting, Hilla Rebay, Guggenheim's adviser and the foundation's first director, selected the renowned American architect Frank Lloyd Wright to design a new building. In a letter to him, Rebay wrote: "I need a fighter, a lover of space, an originator, a tester and a wise man. . . . I want a temple of spirit, a monument!"

- Wright accepted the commission and quickly settled on the idea of a continuous ramp for the main gallery of the museum, as well as sloped walls on which to place paintings. His early schemes show a tremendous variation in forms that he was considering, including a blue glass hexagon and a rose-color marble circular spiral ramp that expands at the bottom rather than at the top, as the final plan does. Guggenheim, who intentionally delayed construction of the building because of postwar inflation, died in 1949.

- In 1956 construction finally began, and the building opened to the public on October 21, 1959, six months after Wright's death. Enormous crowds lined up to experience the architecture, but not all critics recognized its greatness at first. Ada Louise Huxtable, for example, wrote in the *New York Times* that the structure is "less a museum than it is a monument to Frank Lloyd Wright." More recently, critic Paul Goldberger noted that Wright "made it socially and culturally acceptable for an architect to design a highly expressive, intensely personal museum. In this sense almost every museum of our time is a child of the Guggenheim."

- By the 1980s, the repeated annexing of offices in the Wright building for gallery space, and accelerated institutional development, led then-director Thomas Messer to initiate expansion plans. They called for the construction of a tower based on Wright's original design for an eleven-story annex that would serve as a backdrop to the dominant sculptural form of the spiral museum. The addition, designed by Gwathmey Siegel and Associates Architects and completed in 1992, provides more administrative spaces, thus allowing public access to previously restricted portions of the original structure. Four new rectilinear galleries open onto the rotunda's spiral, providing an uninterrupted circulation pattern very much in the spirit of Wright's design.

Thomas Krens

ARCHITECT'S STATEMENT

The following statement by Frank Lloyd Wright is an excerpt from The Solomon R. Guggenheim Museum. Architect: Frank Lloyd Wright *(New York: The Solomon R. Guggenheim Foundation and Horizon Press, 1960).*

The building for the Solomon R. Guggenheim Museum on Fifth Avenue will mark the first advance in the direction of organic architecture, which the great city of New York has to show. Of modern architecture there are a number of examples, of organic architecture, none. It is fortunate that this advanced work appears on the Avenue as a temple of adult education and not as a profit-seeking business-venture.

- Here for the first time architecture appears plastic, one floor flowing into another (more like sculpture) instead of the usual superimposition of stratified layers cutting and butting into each other by way of post-and-beam construction.

- The whole building, cast in concrete, is more like an egg shell—in form a great simplicity—rather than like a criss-cross structure. The light concrete flesh is rendered strong enough everywhere to do its work by embedded filaments of steel either separate or in mesh. The structural calculations are thus those of the cantilever and continuity rather than post and beam. The net result of such construction is a greater repose, the atmosphere of the quiet unbroken wave: no meeting of the eye with abrupt changes of form. All is as one and as near indestructible as it is possible for science to make a building. Unity of design is everywhere present and, naturally enough, the overall simplicity of form and construction ensure a longer life by centuries than that which could be sustained by the skyscraper construction usual in New York City.

- The Solomon R. Guggenheim Museum's walls and spaces, inside and outside, are one in substance and effect. Walls slant gently outward, forming a giant spiral for a well-defined purpose: a new unity between beholder, painting, and architecture. As planned, in the easy downward drift of the viewer on the giant spiral, pictures are not seen to be bolt upright as though painted on the wall behind them. . . . Gently inclined, faced slightly upward to the viewer and to the light in accord with the upward sweep of the spiral, the paintings themselves are emphasized as features in themselves and are not hung "square" but gracefully yield to movement as set up by these slightly curving walls. . . . It remains only to remark upon the degree, quality, and character of the light accorded to various pictures by these unique circumstances. . . . The charm of any work of art, either of painting, sculpture, or architecture, is to be seen in normal, naturally changing light. . . . Seen by daylight to artificial light in naturally varying degree here, also is "three dimensional" light. Instead of light fixed and maintained in two dimensions, this more natural lighting for the nature of a painting is a designed feature of the new Solomon R. Guggenheim Museum.

Northwest corner of Wright building

CRITIC'S COMMENT

Wright's museum did what few other museums even attempted: to become more than a passive frame for the curatorial arts of exhibition and actively to heighten, in an architectural way, the viewer's experience of art shown within it. At every moment, one simultaneously is in intimate proximity to a small group of works yet in the presence of the entire exhibition, large "strips" of which are visible across the room. But perhaps most important is the fact that art exhibitions typically are chronological in structure, and so is the Guggenheim Museum as its spiral path projects the presence of the fourth dimension—time—and shows works of art in an imaginary stream of time past, which physically draws the visitor through it.

Marvin Trachtenberg and Isabelle Hyman,
Architecture: From Prehistory to Postmodernity,
second edition (New York: Abrams, 2002)

Opposite: Interior view, looking up (photo by David Heald © The Solomon R. Guggenheim Foundation)
Above: Top-floor gallery (photo by David Heald © The Solomon R. Guggenheim Foundation)
Left: Detail of façade

HENRY ART GALLERY SEATTLE, WA

Charles Gwathmey

MUSEUM DIRECTOR'S STATEMENT

Founded in 1927, the Henry Art Gallery, operated by the University of Washington, was the first public art museum in the state of Washington and is now the Pacific Northwest's premier modern and contemporary art museum. The Henry engages visitors in the powerful experience of artistic innovation and serves as a catalyst for the creation of new work in the visual arts. The museum also presents exhibitions and programs that re-examine the art of the modern period through the lens of the present. Photography and digital and projected media are of special interest as the Henry explores the vast realm of technological potential in art in the new millennium. The Henry values and encourages experimentation and collaboration as part of the artistic process and as a vital element of the museum's mission.

• The museum's exhibitions bring important works of art to Seattle from throughout the world and bring into public view works of art from the Northwest. These exhibitions and their related programs invite dialogue about contemporary culture, politics, aesthetics, and the traditions of visual art and design of the last two centuries. The Henry has also built a reputation for innovative programming, educational opportunities, and diverse film and lecture series. Building on the rich academic culture of the University of Washington and the supportive and highly involved arts culture of Seattle and the Northwest, the museum fosters collaboration with the public and community groups as well as with students and faculty of the university.

• The museum's major renovation and expansion, completed in April 1997, quadrupled the museum's size, from 10,000 square feet to over 40,000 square feet. Increased size allowed for the addition of a 154-seat auditorium, a multimedia gallery, café, bookstore, and sculpture court, along with improved facilities for art handling and storage and collections research. An architectural collage of glass, textured stainless steel, and cast stone, designed by Charles Gwathmey of Gwathmey, Siegel & Associates, complements the original red-brick collegiate-Gothic structure designed by Carl Gould in the 1920s.

Richard Andrews

ARCHITECT'S STATEMENT

The original Henry Art Gallery, designed by Carl F. Gould in 1927, is a small, elegant masonry structure, the only completed wing of a large arts complex that was planned to serve as the principal gateway to the central campus of the University of Washington.

• In planning an expansion of the space, we determined that it should become a framework for the Gould building, reinforcing the Henry's role as the focal point of that entrance to the campus, enhancing its position in relation to the larger buildings in the vicinity, and realizing the original intentions of the 1927 master plan. To this end, we designed an addition that maintains the unique identity of the Henry, in both its appearance and its function as a museum, and at the same time is responsive to its context.

• To maximize the Henry's site potential, we carved into the hill underneath and around the existing building to accommodate the new three-story structure. It houses exhibition spaces; administrative offices; loading, storage, and preparation areas; and a new lobby, bookstore, and auditorium. The expansion thus fits into the landscape, with the roof of the main gallery becoming a kind of foothill to the campus. This curved slope, which recalls the original site berm, intersects the new pedestrian plaza. The slope maintains a visual depth of field into the central part of the campus referred to as Red Square (because all the buildings and the pavement have been executed in red brick) and the dramatic Suzzallo Library beyond.

• Traditionally, a museum building's interior sequence is ascending, with visitors making their way up through the galleries as they make their discoveries. In the case of the new Henry, the entire sequence of revelation occurs by moving downward. The spaces unfold in the same way that the experience of the collections and exhibitions unveil themselves. By orchestrating the relationship between the building and the collections and exhibitions in this way, the anticipation of reaching each gallery heightens the experience of viewing the art.

• The procession begins at the new entrance off the plaza and continues down a ramp overlooking the new sculpture court and into the renovated galleries of the original building. From there, the visitor moves down to the ground level, arriving at the new contemporary art gallery. At each level, the visitor becomes aware of the interconnection between the existing and the new. From the main skylighted gallery, visitors recall the image of the exterior form and plaza, thus reorienting them to the context of the site.

Charles Gwathmey, Gwathmey, Siegel & Associates

Plaza entrance and pyramid-shape light towers for lower galleries

CRITICS' COMMENTS
Gwathmey, Siegel & Associates, the expansion architects, reversed the tactics they used in their famous expansion of the Guggenheim. . . . Here, the jewel box of the original Henry provides an elegant and versatile sequence of traditional galleries—what Gwathmey, Siegel added were dramatic new spaces which can handle anything from large-scale installations and sculptures to wallworks.
Eric Fredericksen, *The Stranger* (April 24, 1997)

There are places where everything works at the Henry, like an impossibly tall and narrow room carved out of the spiral stair. Bulging ever-so-slightly into the southwest corner of the new main gallery, it is a magical, almost spiritual space, with a distant ceiling that dissolves in light. Occupying this room is like sitting inside a votive candle. By wrapping this sanctified space with a prosaic stair, Gwathmey achieves precisely the kind of collage he seeks, one that enriches each piece through its contrast with the other.
Reed Kroloff, *Architecture Magazine* (September 1997)

Opposite: James Turrell's *Skyspace* gallery
Above: East gallery

Opposite: Upper plaza, showing relationship between museum (left) and campus
Above: South gallery
Left: Entrance to original classical-style building

HOOD MUSEUM OF ART, DARTMOUTH COLLEGE HANOVER, NH

Charles W. Moore / Chad Floyd

MUSEUM DIRECTOR'S STATEMENT

The Hood Museum of Art at Dartmouth College is one of the oldest and most prestigious campus-based museums in the United States. The origins of the permanent collection can be traced back to 1772, when a few natural-science specimens first entered the museum. Collections grew steadily throughout the nineteenth and early twentieth centuries, largely due to the generosity of alumni and friends of the Ivy League institution. These donors were inspired by talented faculty who mounted surprisingly professional displays within academic corridors, at the Old Dartmouth Museum and, after 1929, at the top of Carpenter Hall, home to the art history department.

- In 1962 Wallace K. Harrison's Hopkins Center opened, and an ambitious sequence of temporary exhibitions took place in that modern art center, aided by the hiring of a professional curatorial staff. This multifaceted but fundamentally scattered approach to studying visual culture sufficed until 1981, when Charles W. Moore and Chad Floyd received the commission to create a freestanding, state-of-the-art facility to house the entire breadth of the college collections. An unusual site, sandwiched between the existing Hopkins Center and the campus power plant, was given to the architects, who embraced the eccentricities of this relatively small footprint by producing a narrow, finely detailed structure with dramatic interior spaces and tremendous flexibility. The building, enabled through a gift from longtime college trustee Harvey P. Hood, opened to the public in the fall of 1985.

- Today, the Hood preserves approximately 65,000 individual works of fine art, archaeological materials, and ethnographic objects. The permanent collection aspires to encyclopedic breadth as a support for the college's fundamental teaching mission but also possesses deep strengths in a wide variety of specific culture areas, including Native American, Oceanic, and African collections, old master prints, American colonial silver, and paintings of the White Mountains region of New England.

- The professional museum staff mounts an average of ten temporary exhibitions per year, and since 2001 Dartmouth undergraduate interns have been given curatorial responsibility for a small space dedicated to permanent collection displays. The museum receives an annual average of 45,000 visitors, almost two thirds of them non-academic, and is also proud of its extensive educational outreach, which serves almost 10,000 area elementary and high school students annually. Scholarly lectures and family-oriented programs on weekends make the museum accessible and challenging to campus and local community members. In this way, the Hood Museum of Art aims to live up to the visions of Dartmouth's administration and Charles W. Moore, who from the beginning imagined the institution playing dual roles as an academic research center and a good neighbor to its regional audience.

Derrick R. Cartwright

ARCHITECT'S STATEMENT

The Hood Museum of Art strengthens education in the arts at Dartmouth College, an area that first came into its own in 1962 with the completion of the Hopkins Center for the Performing Arts, designed by Wallace K. Harrison. At 40,000 square feet, the Hood—with twelve art galleries; a 204-seat film and lecture theater; storage, work, and administrative spaces—adds to the Hopkins Center a new building dedicated solely to the fine arts. There are also connectors to several adjacent buildings, notably Harrison's modernist performing arts center and a Romanesque building, Wilson Hall, which has been renovated into performing-arts classrooms.

- The building program required an individual identity for the museum. However, it also asked for a connection to these two flanking structures in order to ensure student exposure to all of the arts and to reduce the effect of inclement weather in this northern climate. It was also desired that the museum have a presence on the Dartmouth Green and that it maintain a public entrance on a street to the south. The museum was configured north–south along the east edge of the site in order to create a wall to hide a nearby heating plant. In the resulting space between the museum and the Hopkins Center, several small courtyards—an idea new to Dartmouth—were created with two connectors.

- In order not to crowd its neighbors while maintaining its own identity, the museum was made to recede, with only a low connector and an outdoor gateway linking Wilson Hall and the Hopkins Center; it is on the other side of this gateway that the Hood Museum rises to its tallest height. Here the museum's turned gable roof and simple brick walls are reminiscent of traditional New England architecture. The museum mediates gently between the Romanesque vigor of Wilson Hall and the modern cleanness of line of the Hopkins Center.

- Inside, the galleries are subordinated to the objects on exhibit. A series of small galleries aligned along the longitudinal axis of the building is reminiscent of the public rooms of great houses for which many of the objects originally were intended. A gallery on the top floor has high walls for the display of large twentieth-century works. Natural light is admitted mostly at circulation points—along the great stairs, at the lobby, and above a catwalk in the twentieth-century gallery from which exhibition lighting is hung.

Chad Floyd, Centerbrook Architects

Southeast side of building

Opposite: Second-floor gallery looking west
Above: Northwest corner of upper gallery

AWARDS

- American Institute of Architects New England, Design Award, 1986
- American Institute of Architects, Honor Award for Architecture, 1987
- Brick in Architecture Award, 1989

CRITICS' COMMENTS

A dignified little museum that fits splendidly into this New England college town. . . . Yet it still exerts a very strong personality of its own.
Ellen Posner, *Wall Street Journal* (November 1, 1985)

It was the building itself that attracted the most attention, not only because it was the star of the [opening] festivities, but because it was obvious to most that it represented a wise and handsome solution to the problems its site and complex functions had presented.
Theodore F. Wolff, *Christian Science Monitor* (October 16, 1985)

The building alludes both to the Georgian architecture of American—and Dartmouth— tradition, and to the modern architecture of the Hopkins Center beside it, and its casual, rather rambling shape pulls the clashing buildings on either side of it into a new and quite remarkable coherence. It is really quite brilliantly sited: one of the few cases anywhere of a large building shoehorned into an awkward space between two other large buildings, and fitting in altogether naturally.
Paul Goldberger, *New York Times* (October 20, 1985)

Opposite: Looking up to second-floor gallery, with different color patterns
Above left: Abstraction of lines and reflections on stairway
Above right: Entrance to main- and upper-level gallery spaces
Left: Looking back to entrance and antiquities galleries

KIMBELL ART MUSEUM FORT WORTH, TX

Louis I. Kahn

MUSEUM DIRECTOR'S STATEMENT

In its short history of some thirty years, the Kimbell Art Museum has come to occupy a distinctive place in the international community of museums. A small collection of fewer than 350 works, acquired at a time when the supply of great masterpieces was thought by many to be drying up, the Kimbell has nonetheless become a byword for quality and importance at the very highest level. Particularly in its holdings of European old and modern master painting—and more selectively in its collections of ancient classical and Egyptian, Asian, African, and Pre-Columbian art—the Kimbell possesses a core of works that epitomize their eras and styles. The works also touch individual high points of aesthetic beauty and historical importance, assuring them a place among the masterpieces of world art. Leaving to older and larger institutions the role of collecting broadly and in depth, the Kimbell has chosen as its primary collecting aspiration the pursuit of quality over quantity.

• Enjoyment and admiration of the Kimbell's collection has, from its inception, been wedded to the equal acclaim accorded the building in which it is housed. Working in close collaboration with its first director, Richard F. Brown, the American architect Louis I. Kahn created for the Kimbell one of the purest and most perfect statements of architectural modernism, a design that is today regarded as one of the finest of all twentieth-century museum designs.

• The signature cycloid-vaulted ceilings; the restrained choice of complementary materials and minimalist interior detailing; the careful articulation of open and enclosed spaces—all these together create what has seemed to many a nearly perfect environment for viewing and contemplating art. This environment is brilliantly mediated by the reflecting pools and planted grove of the entrance and the famously "silvery" light diffused from slits in the cycloids and reflected off the gray concrete vaults. The magic of the Kimbell's galleries has become a celebrated aspect of visiting the museum and a touchstone for many subsequent museum architects, who pay homage to Kahn's design in their own work the world over. (The most recent example is our new neighbor, the Modern Art Museum of Fort Worth, designed by Tadao Ando.)

• As the Kimbell's curator of architecture, Patricia Cummings Loud, has observed: "The unforeseen destiny of the Kimbell Art Museum is the high regard and admiration in which it is held internationally, as an ideal and inspirational museum building." It is this marriage of equals—collection and building—so beautifully attuned to each other that has come to represent the Kimbell's distinctive achievement.

Dr. Timothy F. Potts

ARCHITECT'S STATEMENT

The following are excerpts from the writings of Louis I. Kahn published in the book In Pursuit of Quality: The Kimbell Art Museum *(Fort Worth: Kimbell Art Museum, 1987).*

The institutions of the city are the measure of its character. I am honored to be chosen the architect of the Kimbell Art Museum, which calls for the composition of the spaces housing the collections of the family and the treasures of the world yet to be acquired.

• My mind is full of Roman greatness and the vault so etched itself in my mind that, though I cannot employ it, it's always ready. And the vault seems to be the best. And I realized that the light must come from a high point where the light is best in its zenith. The vault, rising not high, not in an august manner, but somehow appropriate to the size of the individual. And its feeling of being home and safe came to mind.

• Here I felt that the light in the rooms structured in concrete will have the luminosity of silver. I know that rooms for the paintings and objects that fade should only most modestly be given natural light. The scheme of enclosure of the museum is a succession of cycloid vaults, each of a single span 150 feet long and 20 feet wide, each forming the rooms with a narrow slit to the sky, with a mirrored glass shaped to spread natural light on the sides of the vault. This light will give a touch of silver to the room without touching the objects directly, yet give the comforting feeling of knowing the time of day. Added to the skylight from the slit over the exhibit rooms, I cut across the vaults, at a right angle, a counterpoint of courts, open to the sky, of calculated dimensions and character, marking them Green Court, Yellow Court, Blue Court, named for the kind of light that I anticipate their proportions, their foliation, or their sky reflections on surfaces, or on water, will give.

• The entrance of the trees is the entrance by foot, which links Camp Bowie Boulevard and West Lancaster Ave. Two open porticos flank the entrance court of the terrace. In front of each portico is a reflecting pool, which drops its water in a continuous sheet about 70 feet long in a basin two feet below. The sound would be gentle. The stepped entrance court passes between the porticos and their pools with a fountain, around which one sits, on an axis designed to be the source of the portico pools. The west lawn gives the building perspective.

• The south garden is at a level ten feet below the garden entrance, approached by gradual stepped lawns shaped to be a place to sit to watch the performance of a play, music, or dance, the building with its arched silhouette acting as the backdrop of a stage. When not so in use it will seem only as a garden where sculpture acquired from time to time would be.

Southwest corner

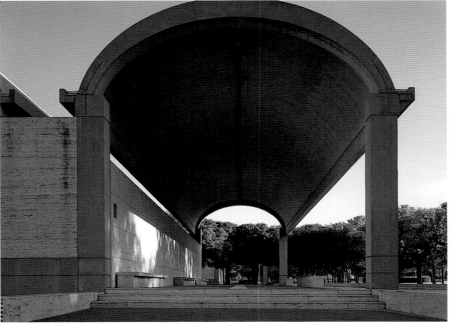

AWARDS

- Best Building Award, National General Contractors Association, 1972
- Award of Excellence, The Art Museum Association, 1982
- Twenty-five Year Award, American Institute of Architects, 1997

CRITIC'S COMMENT

Somewhere between new and old is the Kimbell Art Museum in Fort Worth, the 72-year-old Louis Kahn's first major museum. "When I thought about museums," he says, "I remember that they made me tired as soon as I walked into them." The Kimbell's galleries are small and human-size, and so is the exterior of the museum, a graceful series of cycloid vaults. Informal grouping of chairs and sofas abound. And the lighting at the Kimbell is entirely natural, transmitted by open shafts in the vaults above. "The rapport between a human being and a naturally lit space," says Kahn, "is what architecture is all about." That kind of sensibility gives the Kimbell its distinction in the outburst of museum building in America. **Douglas Davis, *Newsweek*** (September 17, 1973)

Pages 104–5: Exterior of galleries at south end

Opposite: Southwest gallery
Above: South end of southwest gallery
Left: Northwest plaza canopy

THE MENIL MUSEUMS
THE MENIL COLLECTION

Renzo Piano

MUSEUM DIRECTOR'S STATEMENT

The Menil Collection, one of the most unusual and distinguished art museums in the world, opened in 1987 to house, preserve, and exhibit the art collection of philanthropists John and Dominique de Menil. Assembled over many decades, the renowned collection—more than 16,000 paintings, sculptures, prints, drawings, photographs, and rare books—is remarkable for its quality. However, it is also notable for the very personal and yet broad interests of the collectors and for its distinctive presentation in an outstanding architectural setting involving several buildings.

■ After their marriage in France in 1931, the de Menils moved to Houston, Texas, and quickly distinguished themselves in their adopted city by becoming strong advocates of modern art and architecture and supporters of civil and human rights. In the process, they played an outstanding role in bringing modernism to Houston, a city poised to become one of the largest and wealthiest in the United States. Over the years the de Menils commissioned landmark works of architecture and initiated several ambitious research and publishing projects. They also developed plans to build a museum to house their rapidly growing collection of art. Fourteen years after John's death in 1973, Dominique, working with the architect Renzo Piano, fulfilled that dream.

■ The bungalow-style houses around the original museum were to be preserved, and in the 1990s, more satellite buildings were added to the Menil campus, including the Cy Twombly Gallery (1995), also built by Renzo Piano, and the Byzantine Fresco Chapel Museum (1997), by François de Menil. Both of these buildings are discussed on the pages that follow.

■ One of the singular features of the Menil Collection is the underlying principle of dialogue, in which modern and contemporary, local and international works are placed in the context of ancient and more recent world cultures. This dialogue is balanced and enhanced by the human scale and the simplicity of Renzo Piano's architecture and by the parklike surroundings. Both the main building and the Cy Twombly Gallery are masterpieces of understatement. Although built according to highest standards, the technical installations do not interfere with the museum's essential atmosphere of contemplation.

■ John and Dominique de Menil left a remarkable legacy to Houston and to the world. As the holdings of the Menil Collection continue to grow, it will be a vital part of Houston's cultural life, an international art destination, and a home for the distinctive presentation of high-quality art and its encounter with diverse audiences.

Josef Helfenstein

ARCHITECT'S STATEMENT

The Menil Collection is made up of more than 16,000 works of primitive and modern art, only some of which are on display at any given time, in a setting illuminated mainly by natural light. The museum is a complex space, enriched by the pattern of multiple planes and the invasion of nature. It embodies the vision of a museum village.

■ The museum was designed at the behest of Dominique de Menil, who wished to create an experimental museum that would consist of a restoration workshop, art galleries, and a village, while drawing upon the widest possible use of natural light.

■ The works in the collection are displayed on a rotating basis, and those not on exhibition are stored in the Treasure House on the second level (a protected, climate-controlled site separated from the first-level exhibition galleries). By exhibiting the works for short periods of time, it is possible to expose them temporarily to higher-than-normal levels of light, of about 1000 lux.

■ The roof of the museum is made of leaflike modular elements that allow light to pour in but that filter out ultraviolet rays. The transfusion of zenithal light through these leaves gives the rooms a unique character, different at each moment, depending on the position of the sun. In keeping with this effect, the museum's repeated spaces and multiple planes (the galleries open out to interior gardens) contribute to the sense of a vibrating light and to the overall feeling of lightness. Hence, the museum becomes a place for calm and tranquil contemplation.

■ The museum is surrounded by trees, lawns, and traditional houses typical of Houston's historic district. Some of these houses serve as museum annexes for specific activities (book shop, administration, and so on). The main building is modeled on the style of these houses, echoing their motifs or drawing on the same construction methods or materials. Without dominating and overshadowing the district, the museum fits in with its surroundings, like a museum village.

■ Mrs. de Menil commissioned a permanent wing, which was constructed in 1992, devoted to the work of Cy Twombly. This second museum has a stricter, more defined, and discrete structure: it, too, avoids dominating the other houses. The artist wanted a square space that would be extremely simple, even spare, illuminated by light that was omnipresent but less direct than in the other museum and more diffuse (at an intensity of about 300 lux).

Renzo Piano, Renzo Piano Building Workshop

North façade

CRITICS' COMMENTS

She [Dominique de Menil] has created what is probably the finest and least pompous museum of the 1980s. Curiously, and for several reasons, one reaches for the word Gothic in trying to describe the nature of this very natural building. First, the building has the feel of American Carpenter's Gothic; its simple steel and timber construction echoes the wooden balloon-frame houses surrounding it.... Second, the elegant cast concrete "leafs" that baffle the dazzling Texan sunlight and which completely cover the galleries are like some modern Gothic vaulting. Third, the building has been put together by a genuinely interdisciplinary team. The engineers (Ove Arup & Partners) have contributed as much as the architect's (Renzo Piano's Building Workshop), and the local executive architects (Fitzgerald of Houston).
Jonathan Glancey, *The Architect* (September 1987)

Some 300 overlapping ferro-concrete panels designed by Mr. Piano and his engineering associate, Peter Rice, reflect and refract light coming in through the glass roof. Direct sunlight is filtered out and the effect is like walking beneath the canopy of a majestic, leafy, and disease-proof elm. Depending on the weather outside, the atmosphere inside can be moody, sunny, or downright sullen. This natural effect permitted by the ferro-concrete "foliage" allows the Menil Collection to avoid the usual hospital feel of museums hermetically sealed off from the outside world and displaying art like embalmed specimens in 'The Twilight Zone' under artificial light.
Manuela Hoelterhoff, *The Wall Street Journal*
(June 16, 1987)

Opposite: Southwestern galleries
Above: Oceanic art gallery, with tropical planting atrium banking north end
Left: Southwest corner, showing second-floor Treasure House

THE ROTHKO CHAPEL

Opposite: Interior of the Rothko Chapel
(photo © Hickey-Robertson, Houston)
Above: Interior of Cy Twombly Gallery
Left: Light-controlling louvers on roof of Cy Twombly Gallery

CY TWOMBLY GALLERY

BYZANTINE FRESCO CHAPEL MUSEUM

François de Menil

FOUNDATION PRESIDENT'S STATEMENT

The Byzantine Fresco Chapel Museum was opened to the public in February 1997. Its mission is to present its thirteenth-century frescoes, dome, and, apse—the only examples of this significance and size in North America—in a manner that returns them to their original religious function as sacred art. As a part of a larger campus, the museum completes an important function in relation to the Rothko Chapel, the Menil Collection, and the Cy Twombly Gallery in allowing the whole to be understood as a modern-day sanctuary founded on the ideas of art and spirituality.

- In June 1983, the Menil Foundation, the museum's parent organization, was shown photographs of thirteenth-century frescoes from a small votive chapel near Lysi, in Turkish-occupied Cyprus. The frescoes had been cut into thirty-eight pieces and removed from their original site, to be sold individually for profit and dispersed. Struck by the beauty of the works, the Menil Foundation, through its legal representatives, sought to find the true country of origin of the work. Through painstaking efforts, it was learned that the Church of Cyprus was the owner of the works, so the foundation purchased the frescoes on their behalf and restored them to wholeness. In return, the Church of Cyprus granted the foundation a long-term loan of the art.

- Dominique de Menil, the museum's founder, remarked on seeing the mural pieces: "If someone is drowning in front of you, and though you can hardly swim, you are tempted to jump into the water. . . . A masterpiece would have disappeared. Worse, their true function of sacred images, of great icons, would be lost forever. So, we jumped."

- Today the Byzantine Fresco Chapel Museum is a site for study, meditation, and reflection for the thousands who visit it each year.

Susan de Menil

ARCHITECT'S STATEMENT

In the program statement, Dominique de Menil outlined her unique approach to the display of spiritual antiquities: "For the first time, important fragments of a religious building are not considered only as antiquities. They are approached also as relics and consideration is given to their religious nature. . . . A typical museum presentation leaves out an intangible element, difficult to weigh and express, yet very real. It leaves out their spiritual importance and betrays their original significance." The new chapel had to return the frescoes to their original religious function, as well as bring transcendence to their tragic past by a new context with new meaning. The chapel is not only a place of worship for the Orthodox rite, but also a place of contemplation where people of all faiths can experience peace and the communality of spiritual belief. It is simultaneously a lament and a celebration of the human spirit.

- A re-creation of the original chapel at Lysi would have been contextually inappropriate in a contemporary city such as Houston. It would also have resulted in the creation of more "replica" than real, thereby diminishing the importance of the frescoes. The chapel's design addresses the transposition of the ancient relics to the contemporary site by means of a mediating concrete external building with an embedded steel structure: a reliquary box. A reliquary box derives from the tradition of housing sacred objects in small casketlike cases, sometimes one within another.

- The dislocation/relocation of the sacred works is addressed through an inversion. The ethereal soul is solidified and made opaque in the frescoes. The material solidity of the original chapel building is shattered and made ephemeral by means of the fragmented freestanding glass structure. Twentieth-century steel technology supports this fractured body and transposes it to an active present. The "immaterial" materiality of the infill glass panels intensifies the absence/presence of the original site.

- The sense of beyond, characteristic of all religions, is evoked through the play of darkness and light. The light at the center is surrounded by darkness, which itself is again surrounded by light.

François de Menil

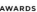

AWARDS
- AIA Honor Award, Architecture, 1999
- AIA New York City Project Award, 1994

CRITICS' COMMENTS

The Byzantine Fresco Chapel is an abstract version of a 13th-century building set within a 20th-century box, a place where the architecture of the 20th century honors that of the 13th not by creating a fake 13th-century environment, and not by parodying the past or trivializing it, but by using the tools and shapes of today, respectfully.

Manuela Hoelterhoff, *The Wall Street Journal* (June 16, 1987)

Usually, Byzantine chapels and churches were decorated top to bottom with murals. De Menil has simply extended the effect murals always had on church walls by dematerializing the rest of the chapel with darkness and light. He created an interior with a double revelation—the murals themselves, and then the light that dematerializes and transcends matter, becoming an object itself. The chapel progresses from stone to concrete and climaxes in luminance.

Joseph Giovannini, *Architecture* (April 1997)

Left: Byzantine Fresco Chapel
Above: Frescoes

MILWAUKEE ART MUSEUM

Eero Saarinen, David Kahler, Santiago Calatrava

MUSEUM DIRECTOR'S STATEMENT

The collections of the Milwaukee Art Museum include more than 20,000 works spanning antiquity to the present day. The museum's primary strengths are in nineteenth- and twentieth-century American and European art, contemporary art, American decorative arts, old master paintings, and folk and self-taught art. Founded in 1888, the Layton Art Gallery merged with the Milwaukee Art Institute in 1957 and formed the Milwaukee Art Center, which was renamed the Milwaukee Art Museum in 1980.

- The museum's 1954–57 building, with 160,000 square feet, was designed by Eero Saarinen, and in 1975, an addition to house the Bradley collection of modern art was built by Kahler, Fitzhugh, and Scott. In 1994 Santiago Calatrava began work on the Quadracci Pavilion, which was completed in October 2001 and named by *Time* magazine "Best Design of 2001." Elegant public gardens were designed by noted landscape architect Dan Kiley. The museum's 2001 expansion, with 140,000 square feet, provided a 30 percent increase in overall gallery space, enhanced educational and public programming facilities, and expanded public amenities.

- More than 500,000 people visited the Milwaukee Art Museum during its first full year of operation after the new building opened. Signature elements of the Calatrava design include the Reiman Bridge, a 250-foot-long suspended pedestrian bridge that links downtown Milwaukee directly to the lakefront and the museum. The main entrance leads into a parabola-shape, glass-enclosed reception hall with a 90-foot-high ceiling. The Burke Brise-Soleil—a moveable, winglike sunscreen comprising seventy-two steel fins, rests on top of the glass-enclosed reception hall and is raised and lowered to control both temperature and light in the structure.

- The museum's selection committee searched for over a year for the architect of the new building. The committee focused on international candidates whose work would be compatible with the existing structures and who were capable of a strong architectural statement. Also required was an architect who had demonstrated the capacity for designing exciting yet functional public buildings and who had an international reputation and recognition. The initial list of candidates numbered more than seventy. Santiago Calatrava, a Spaniard with architectural offices in Zurich, Paris, and Valencia, met all of the museum's criteria. His work was recognized throughout the world for its innovation, integrity, and functionality, and his designs for buildings throughout Europe had won many international design competitions. The Milwaukee Art Museum addition was his first building completed in the United States.

David Gordon

ARCHITECT'S STATEMENT

For me, the project of expanding the Milwaukee Art Museum was an opportunity to help people make the most of an extraordinary situation. They had the institution, first of all, with its dramatic, original building by Eero Saarinen, which is very strong and whose integrity had been preserved by David Kahler's understated extension. They had the topography of the city, which descends to Lake Michigan from hilltop terraces. And, of course, they had the whole sweep of the shore, looking out as far as the horizon.

- These were the invaluable assets that the people of Milwaukee entrusted to me. And they offered me something else as well, which is absolutely crucial for any architect. In the trustees of the Milwaukee Art Museum, I had clients who truly wanted from me the best architecture that I could do. Their ambition was to create something exceptional for their community.

- So the design did not result from a sketch. It came out of a close collaboration with the clients, who enthusiastically accepted the key idea that emerged from our discussions. Instead of adding something more to the Saarinen building, I proposed to add something to the lakefront.

- The extension, as such, is a kind of pavilion, transparent and light, which contrasts with the massive, compact Saarinen building. Reaching out from the Quadracci Pavilion, like an arm extended to the city, is a bridge. I thought this design might establish a pattern of events for possible future additions—a bridge to the city and a very shallow pavilion that interrupts the view of the lake as little as possible.

- Besides being a link to the city, the bridge is part of a composition. Its leaning mast conveys a sense of direction, of movement, which is taken up by the roof, the cables, and the canopies that extend on each side. These strong lines culminate in the Burke Brise-Soleil, which translates their dynamism into actual motion. In the crowning element of the *brise-soleil*, the building's form is at once formal (completing the composition), functional (controlling the level of light), symbolic (opening to welcome visitors), and iconic (creating a memorable image for the museum and the city).

- I hope that people visiting the new Milwaukee Art Museum will feel that we have designed not a building, but a piece of the city.

Santiago Calatrava

East façade on Lake Michigan

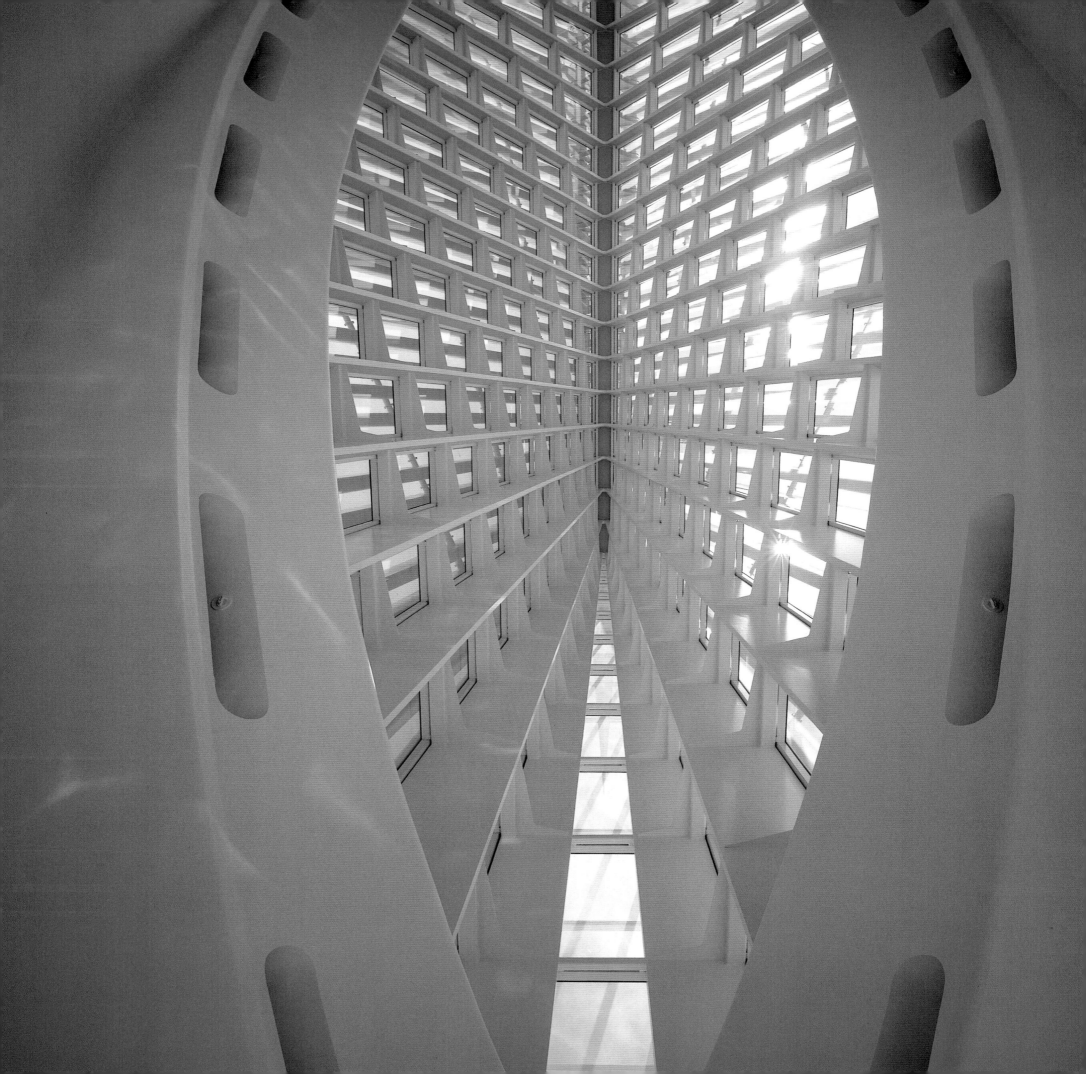

CRITIC'S COMMENT

It is a kind of urban event, and one of the most pleasing exercises in structural exhibitionism in a long time. . . . This is Calatrava's first building in the United States, and it bears some resemblance to American architecture that he admires, particularly Eero Saarinen's T.W.A. Terminal at Kennedy Airport. The interior of the reception hall is an homage to that building, with the same swooping space, but it is lighter and more graceful. Calatrava is a lyricist. His architecture soars, and it celebrates light, transparency, and soft, sensuous curves.

Paul Goldberger, *The New Yorker* (November 5, 2001)

Opposite: View of ceiling in reception hall
Above left: East side of main entrance hall
Above right: Bridge to museum (wings are opened and extended when wind speeds are safe)
Left: Looking toward reception hall, with Dale Chihuly sculpture at right

Pages 120–21: East Galleria at twilight

MODERN ART MUSEUM OF
FORT WORTH FORT WORTH, TX

Tadao Ando

MUSEUM DIRECTOR'S STATEMENT

Twenty women established the Modern Art Museum of Fort Worth in 1892, when the state of Texas was only forty-seven years old. It is the oldest art museum in the state of Texas and one of the oldest museums in the western United States.

• The Modern Art Museum is dedicated to collecting, presenting, and interpreting international developments in post-World War II art in all media. The Modern promotes interest in art and artists through curatorial research and publications and a variety of educational programs, including lectures, guided tours, classes, and workshops. From 1954, the museum was located in the 39,000-square-foot Fort Worth Art Center designed by Herbert Bayer; in 1974, O'Neil Ford & Associates designed an expansion, but space was very limited for a growing institution.

• Following the purchase of 10.96 acres of land by the Burnett Foundation in the late 1990s, six world-class architects were asked to create design proposals for the new museum. The design created by Tadao Ando Architect & Associates of Osaka, Japan, was the unanimous choice of the building committee. Mr. Ando, one of the most renowned architects in the world, has received all of architecture's consummate prizes. His design is a work of modern art in itself, based on his vision of the building as a swan upon a lake. With forty-foot-high glass walls framed in metal and surrounded by concrete, the building sits on a one-and-a-half-acre reflecting pond. Supporting the concrete roof are forty-foot-tall concrete Y-shape columns.

• Construction began in the fall of 1999 and was completed in August 2002 at a cost of $65 million. On December 14, 2002, the new museum was unveiled to the public. Mr. Ando's design enabled the museum to expand its gallery space from 9,917 to 53,000 square feet. The galleries are divided into two floors, which allows the museum's staff to display works from the important permanent collection on one floor while hosting a major traveling exhibition on the other.

• The collection consists of more than 2,600 significant works of modern and contemporary art, including works by Jackson Pollock, Anselm Kiefer, and Andy Warhol. Through this new building, the staff and trustees of the Modern hope to welcome visitors into the world of modern and contemporary art. The Modern stands not only as a reflection in the water but also as a reflection of the cultural community that has come to exist in Fort Worth, Texas, and that continues to grow.

Dr. Marla Price

ARCHITECT'S STATEMENT

This project is located on the outskirts of downtown Fort Worth, Texas. The site is a large park of 480,000 square feet, just one road away from a masterwork of twentieth-century architecture—the Kimbell Art Museum designed by Louis I. Kahn. Thus, one major issue of my design is its relationship with the Kimbell. I attempted to extract the essence of his simple and clear spaces and imbue the new architecture with its strength.

• I have conceived my project as an "Arbor for the Art," a concept indicating that every part of this extensive site is conceived as an environment for the unhurried appreciation of art. The building consists of a series of five rectangular concrete boxes in a parallel arrangement, each box being sheathed in a skin of glass. Although the overall configuration of the layout appears simple, a multitude of different places and volumes are provided for the exhibition spaces, with further variety added by the use of several different natural lightning systems.

• The material strength of the concrete protects the priceless artworks housed within the museum from the extremes of the local climate. The interior concrete boxes assure structural security, and the exterior glass boxes filter the direct influence of the external climate on the exhibition spaces. Glass and concrete are two materials representative of this century. Sheathed within their glass skins, the concrete parallelepipeds emphasize the transparency of the glass, while the glass softens the strong impression that would be created by the exposure of massive forms.

• I then arranged a wide water garden on the eastern part of the site, where the tranquil natural environment is shielded from the road traffic by a grove of trees. While making rooms appropriate for an ideal display of works of art, my strategy was to dilute any strict border between interior and exterior. The mediating spaces enclosed between the glass skins and the massive concrete walls of each pavilion are like the *engawa* space of Japanese traditional architecture, belonging to both interior and exterior. They are integral parts of the exhibition spaces and stimulate the visitor's spirit while incorporating the light, water, and greenery of the surrounding landscape.

• My intention was to provide a truly open museum, one that will serve as a refreshing oasis in the midst of the severe local climate, an arbor of peace to stimulate the spirit of creativity.

Tadao Ando, Tadao Ando Architect & Associates

South-gallery building seen in reflecting pool from café patio

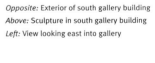

Opposite: Exterior of south gallery building
Above: Sculpture in south gallery building
Left: View looking east into gallery

Drawn by rave reviews in the press and by word of mouth, devotees of art and architecture are streaming here to visit the new home of the Modern Art Museum of Fort Worth. . . . The building causing this commotion stands 40 feet tall and dominates a windswept 11-acre site on the edge of town. Tadao Ando, the celebrated Japanese architect who designed it, has grabbed attention for Fort Worth the way Frank Gehry did for Bilbao, Spain, after his Guggenheim Museum opened six years ago. The two buildings could not be more different. Gehry's is wild, shiny, and curved. Ando's is stately, serene, and meditative.

Stephen Kinzer, *New York Times* (January 29, 2003)

Ando's strategy for organizing the new building is partly based on the (adjacent) Kimbell, with calm parallel gallery spaces, lit as far as possible by daylight and opening on to nature (in the Kahn building exquisitely planted courts, but in the Ando the much larger new park). . . . For all the similarities, there are very significant differences between the two buildings. Kahn's galleries are reminiscent of Cistercian vaults in their awesome simplicity. Ando's exhibition spaces are concrete boxes within glass ones. The heavy inner boxes are the main containers for the artworks, while the glass ones provide intermediate spaces between galleries and the lake and lawns.

■ The other major difference between Ando and Kahn is that Ando (for all the size of his site) found it necessary to put his galleries on two levels. One of the reasons for this must surely be the difference in scale between much contemporary work and the paintings in the Kimbell, which contains a fundamentally private collection of works of easel and domestic scale. . . . Ando has exploited the possibilities of the two levels of galleries with sudden surprising juxtapositions of volume and scale, but the arrangement means that lower, single-height galleries must inevitably seem slightly second class because they cannot receive daylight.

Robert Morant, *Architectural Review* (August 2003)

Sculpture and skyline from north gallery building

MUSEUM OF CONTEMPORARY ART CHICAGO, IL

Josef Paul Kleihues

MUSEUM DIRECTOR'S STATEMENT

The Museum of Contemporary Art in Chicago was opened as a *kunsthalle* in October 1967 by a group of culturally concerned residents who recognized the need for an internationally oriented forum for contemporary art in the city. Within six years, the museum had made a commitment to building a permanent collection, and by 1979, the MCA had expanded into an adjacent townhouse, which included 11,000 square feet of exhibition space. In 1992, the MCA selected from an international field of two hundred applicants the Berlin-based architect Josef Paul Kleihues to design its new building and sculpture garden, his first commission in the United States. The new building opened in July 1996 with nearly seven times the square footage of the museum's previous facility, and for the first time the MCA has space to install temporary exhibitions and works from its collection simultaneously.

▪ Our mission at the MCA is to be an innovative and compelling center of contemporary art, where the public can directly experience the work and ideas of living artists and understand the historical, social, and cultural context of the art of our time. We boldly interweave exhibitions, performances, collections, and educational programs to excite, challenge, and illuminate our visitors and to provide insight into the creative process. Devoted to presenting the art of our time, the MCA offers exhibitions and a collection of the most thought-provoking art created since 1945. The collection of 5,600 works features notable strengths in Surrealism, Minimalism, Post-Minimalism, conceptual photography, and works by Chicago-based artists.

▪ Our performance programs feature some of the most influential artists working today in performance, music, dance, and media arts. Most of the first floor is dedicated to education facilities, as the MCA is committed to engaging a broad and diverse audience in a wide variety of educational programs. The MCA also boasts a gift shop, bookstore, restaurant, 300-seat theater, and terraced sculpture garden overlooking Lake Michigan.

▪ In a city known for its architecture, the MCA stands as a brilliant showcase for contemporary art, sensitive to its surroundings yet bold enough to stand alone as art. In keeping with the space designed to offer an environment for "concentrated and undisturbed contemplation of works of art," we fine-tuned the galleries by installing black terrazzo flooring and new spot lighting to create a synthesized and understated backdrop for the art, with an eye to the detail that is integral to the vision of the MCA.

Robert Fitzpatrick

ARCHITECT'S STATEMENT

I was asked what I found particularly appealing about the chance to build in Chicago. The answer to this is very simple. The great appeal lies in the architectonic culture, which has shaped this city's image. You find many elements in cast iron and cast bronze in the Chicago School of architecture, especially in buildings done by Adler and Sullivan. I also know a number of buildings in Chicago where the window frames are cast aluminum. So there was a reason to come back to that tradition—not just to imitate it, but also really to use a material that has a strong evocative power.

▪ I wanted to come back to the straight and strong image of the Chicago building, which has integrity not only as a design but also as a piece of construction. For the same reason, I wanted a façade with no real ornaments, but I wanted a structure that would remember the tradition of ornaments in Chicago—the very beautiful terra-cotta elements you find in Adler and Sullivan's buildings. The pyramidal structure of the cast aluminum panels carries with it that memory. Finally, I wanted to do something that would remind us not only of the power of Chicago architecture but also of the tradition of craftsmanship. You can see how the cast aluminum panels are fixed on the building, with steel pins. The elements of the façade have a precise modular order, but you can see the building was made in a very normal way. That's something else the façade is telling people.

▪ I wanted a building that had a chance to get old. It shouldn't look new after five or ten years. It should change its face, its character, over time. I also hope the lake side of the building will look different after a while from the Pearson face, which will look different from the Michigan Avenue face. The warmth of weathering Indiana limestone next to the patina of the cast aluminum will look fantastic!

▪ Louis Sullivan located various functional elements with complete freedom, placing them at will along the sides of the rectangle. The organization is totally free and totally functional. You'd never find that in Europe—the way Sullivan just plugs in the elements however he wants. That's very Chicago. The MCA is also a basic shape, a square in this case, with seven bays on each side. I used the corners to plug in almost everything we needed for vertical installation—elevators, staircases, and so forth. Then, centered in the front, you have the grand entrance, which is three bays wide and two bays deep, leading to the axis that runs straight through from west to east. That's the whole system.

▪ When I plan a garden, I always try to create a difference between the garden and the building. The MCA building is a tough, clear, geometric organization. The sculpture garden has a number of geometric elements, but it is free composition, so there is always a dialogue between garden and building.

Josef Paul Kleihues

West façade with temporary outdoor exhibition

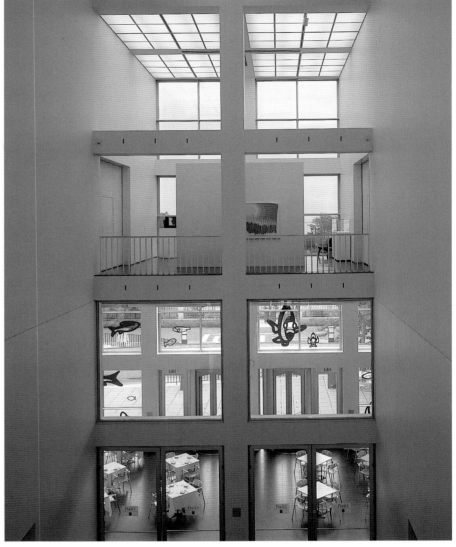

CRITICS' COMMENTS

When applied in the form of smooth sheets (usually colored black), aluminum has long been common dress for buildings and has cloaked everything up to such giants as John Hancock Center and Sears Tower. Kleihues's choice of square cast aluminum panels is another matter, however, because the casting process will give the metal a textured finish that will reflect light quite differently. Moreover, Kleihues plans on using aluminum in its natural, pewterlike color, figuring in time it will acquire an interesting new patina. He intends to leave exposed—but flush with the surface—the heads of hundreds of bolts holding the panels to the building frame. The bolt pattern will establish a micro-modular order.
Paul Gapp, *Chicago Tribune* (March 29, 1992)

Interplay between containment and transparency is the guiding concept behind this building, and it pays off with often stunning results. From the outside, the building is blockily opaque. The building's central bay, aligned with the grand staircase, is encased by glass. But the view of the interior scarcely prepares you for the amplitude of space that opens up when you cross the threshold. An atrium soars four stories overhead, a vista of the lake beckons you forward, but the real shock comes when you pivot around and gaze back toward the entrance. The view of the city is as startling as a magician's trick—who put that there?—and it becomes even more impressive as you explore the building's upper levels.
Herbert Muschamp, *New York Times* (June 30, 1996)

Page 130: Third-floor southwest gallery
Page 131: Looking up stairwell to skylight

Opposite: View toward main entrance from north stairwell
Above left: Front hall to galleries and restaurant
Above right: View toward east end from third-floor balcony

MUSEUM OF CONTEMPORARY ART

LOS ANGELES, CA

Frank O. Gehry, Arata Isozaki

MUSEUM DIRECTOR'S STATEMENT

In 1979, a small group of private citizens joined together with artists, collectors, and museum professionals worldwide to establish a contemporary art museum in Los Angeles. MOCA's founders commissioned two of the world's most renowned and respected architects, Arata Isozaki and Frank O. Gehry, to design its two primary facilities: MOCA at California Plaza, located on historic Bunker Hill in downtown Los Angeles, and MOCA at The Geffen Contemporary in the city's Little Tokyo district.

- MOCA at California Plaza was the result of a progressive development initiative, made possible by both public- and private-sector support, which allocated public art funds to incorporate a museum into a mixed-use real estate development. The museum's architecture committee selected Isozaki after an exhaustive international search, and in 1983 the groundbreaking for his innovative building began. His distinctive plan situated the galleries below ground to reduce the bulk of the building, opting to make a more human-scale collection of geometric forms to contrast with the soaring height of the surrounding skyscrapers. As a result, the California Plaza museum is like an oasis or small village amid the massive towers. Completed in 1986, MOCA's California Plaza complex contains 25,000 square feet of pristine, classically-scaled gallery space, and 75,000 square feet given over to staff offices, an auditorium, art storage, a bookstore, a café, and, nestled in the center, a sculpture plaza.
- In the meantime, MOCA received an extraordinary opportunity to convert a former police car garage in Little Tokyo into a temporary exhibition facility. Known as the Temporary Contemporary, this 55,000-square-foot building offered unlimited opportunities for the presentation of ambitious art and comprehensive exhibitions. Frank Gehry's visionary concept for adaptive reuse sparked a trend toward a "warehouse" aesthetic and the subsequent repurposing of existing buildings by such museums as the Tate Modern, MASS MoCA, and DIA Beacon. After opening in 1983, it soon became a permanent facility named MOCA at The Geffen Contemporary.
- The Museum of Contemporary Art has evolved into a significant international art destination, distinguished for its buildings, collections, exhibitions, educational initiatives, scholarship, and public programs. Devoted to art created since 1940, MOCA has assembled one of the most acclaimed collections in the world, comprising approximately five thousand works in all mediums, ranging from masterpieces of Abstract Expressionism and Pop Art to groundbreaking works by younger and emerging artists. With two such magnificent and flexible venues, MOCA is able to fulfill its mandate—collecting and presenting the best and most progressive art of our time.

Jeremy Strick

ARCHITECT'S STATEMENT

The Museum of Contemporary Art in Los Angeles was my first major commission in the United States. In MOCA's design, I employed not one but several basic geometric forms—pyramid, cylinder, cube. Using these forms of technology as a vocabulary and in 1997, I added a striking canopy, a "translucent cloud," suspended above the ARCO courtyard.

- I think the main room of the building is the best in the gallery, nothing else. If a museum cannot get good galleries, that is a very bad building in my opinion. This building is not for classical art, but for contemporary art, so I tried hard to expand the possibilities for the artists to install their works in that space. Maybe when an artist sees the rooms, he can develop his imagination in that space or environment. The interior has to be a backdrop.
- The interior was spread over seven levels and comprised seven interconnecting galleries (approximately 24,500 square feet of exhibition space), an auditorium, bookstore, café, sculpture court, staff offices, library, support service areas, and storage spaces for MOCA's permanent collection.
- The interior must be a backdrop to the art, but the exterior must have some specific character, a symbolic character. The symbolism of the building is not related to its volume. It is surrounded by gigantic buildings and is, in a sense, in the middle of the valley of the skyscrapers. So the museum building has to be a small object that attracts people's attention, not with its volume but with its materials and forms. That's why I broke the building into fragments—little pyramids, the vault, small cubes. These elements are facing each other and, in a way, look like a small village inside the valley created by the skyscrapers.
- Use of the exterior materials of red Indian sandstone, red granite, dark-green aluminum, crystallized glass, and copper all serve to accentuate the building's geometric forms, most of which perch atop the architectural boxes containing galleries and offices. These include eleven pyramid-shape skylights, one vast saw-tooth skylight covering over 6,800 square feet of gallery space, the barrel vault, a cube on top of the administrative wing, and the square-shape ticket booth.
- Among the greatest challenges was the site itself, which stretches 340 feet along Grand Avenue, a split-level thoroughfare. I positioned the museum's service level entrance on lower Grand Avenue and designed a dramatic public entranceway, formed by the underside of the 53-foot-high, barrel-vaulted library structure, to front upper Grand Avenue.

Arata Isozaki

East end from south plaza

CRITIC'S COMMENT

Mr. Isozaki's architecture is based on groups of simple basic geometric forms, which he places with a delicate, sculptural precision. . . . Approaching the building brings more pleasure than seeing art inside it—its great barrel-vaulted library, which leaps over the entrance to become the top of a formal gateway, and the series of glass pyramids that light the galleries give the museum a spectacular profile. . . . The exterior of the building is exquisitely crafted. The deep red sandstone, wisely left in a rough finish, becomes even more sensual the closer we are to it; the other materials, which include some glass block, some walls of dark green enamel with a crosshatching pattern of pink lines and stainless steel sign panels by Chermayeff & Geismar, play off against the sandstone with just the right amount of contrast. The mix of pink and green in the metal side walls is much less frivolous than it sounds; like much of Mr. Isozaki's work, it represents an exquisite balance between the exuberant and the disciplined, between the spirited and the formal.
Paul Goldberger, *New York Times* (October 26, 1966)

Opposite: Entrance lobby
Above left: Northeast corner gallery
Above right: Frank Gehry sculpture in west side gallery, showing pyramid light well
Left: East exterior from sub-plaza entrance

Pages 138–39: West building in context of downtown skyscrapers

MUSEUM OF FINE ARTS, HOUSTON HOUSTON, TX

William Ward Watkin, Kenneth Franzheim, Ludwig Mies van der Rohe, S. I. Morris, Rafael Moneo

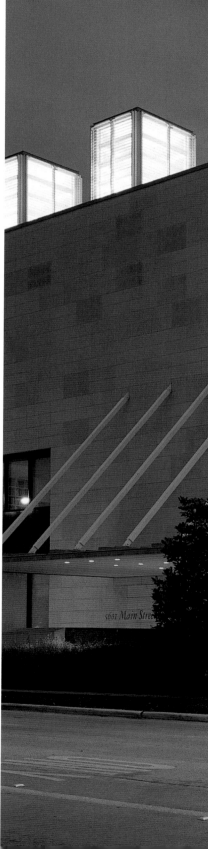

MUSEUM DIRECTOR'S STATEMENT

Founded in 1924, the Museum of Fine Arts, Houston (MFAH), is the largest art museum in America south of Chicago, west of Washington, D.C., and east of Los Angeles. The collection contains more than 45,000 artworks, which date from antiquity to the present. More than two million people visit the MFAH each year, and community outreach programs touch the lives of more than 670,000 people.

- MFAH has a distinguished history of commissioning leading architects to design its buildings. In 1924 William Ward Watkin developed architectural plans in the popular Neoclassical style for the original building. The Robert Lee Blaffer Memorial Wing, designed by Kenneth Franzheim, opened in 1953, and that same year the MFAH retained Mies van der Rohe to create a master plan for the institution. He designed two additions to the complex—Cullinan Hall, completed in 1958, and the Brown Pavilion, completed in 1974. A renowned example of the International Style, the Caroline Wiess Law Building, where modern and non-Western works of art are exhibited in grand, open galleries, is one of only two Mies-designed museums in the world.
- In 1979 the Glassell School of Art, designed by S. I. Morris Associates, opened to the public. Created by Isamu Noguchi, the Lillie and Hugh Roy Cullen Sculpture Garden was completed in 1986. Praised as the most beautiful acre in Houston, the garden houses more than thirty masterworks from the MFAH and other major collections. It also unites the pathways between the Law Building and the school.
- Designed by architect Rafael Moneo, the Audrey Jones Beck Building opened to acclaim in March 2000, the first major American museum commission for Moneo, who received in 1996 architecture's highest honor, the Pritzker Prize. Two specially commissioned, monumental bronze reliefs by Joseph Havel, entitled *Curtain,* flank the building's principal entrance, welcoming you to the MFAH's newest architectural masterpiece.
- The Beck Building lobby leads into a soaring, light-filled atrium, from which visitors can access the galleries on the other floors. Antiquities and European art are presented in twenty-eight classically designed galleries on the second floor. Galleries for prints, drawings, photographs, and American art and a sculpture court reaching more than seventy feet to its skylighted roof, as well as a grand atrium for classical art, are located on the first floor. A tunnel sculpture by James Turrell (*The Light Inside*) joins the Beck and Law Buildings at the lower level.

Peter C. Marzio

ARCHITECT'S STATEMENT

The Museum of Fine Arts Houston was built in 1924 to the design of William Ward Watkin, and Ludwig Mies van der Rohe later built extensions, first in 1958 and again in 1974. It is enough to say that the architecture of Mies has prevailed and that today the modest and dignified architecture of the original museum building has been absorbed into the severe and dark metal framework of the German master.

- A new building for the museum, the Audrey Jones Beck Building, designed to provide additional exhibit spaces for the collections, is joined to the actual museum by an underground exhibition gallery passage. This building cannot be considered an extension, however, but is a separate and autonomous structure. In spite of the apparent homogeneity of the street grid in which it is built, my study of the neighborhood made me appreciate certain characteristics of the site. Therefore, the orientation of the new building was the first design decision, and so the Beck Building opens onto Main Street, a popular thoroughfare in the city.
- However, it must be said that in Houston buildings are perceived from the automobile, thus a frontal view of a building, which can be experienced by those on foot, is simply not possible. So the Beck Building occupies nearly all its site, which gave us an opportunity to explore the potential of a compact structure built within tight confines. Compact architecture clearly demonstrates how it is possible to break down a regular surface into a series of figures that define rooms and corridors, stairs and openings, galleries and light courts, and so on. Compact architecture gives rise to saturated, dense floor plans that make use of the interstitial spaces to encourage movement and can permit surprising liberty in the disposition of architectural programs.
- MFAH is a clear example of this way of understanding architecture. Thus the floor plan of the museum is broken into a whole series of rooms and galleries connected by means of a hidden path that guides the visitor's steps without being imperious. The museum makes intense use of natural light to illuminate the rooms and galleries from above. The variety of the gallery spaces is reflected in the broken outline of the roof, which becomes the most characteristic image of the museum. This shows the importance given to the light, the real protagonist of an architecture whose substance is found in the interior space.

Rafael Moneo

Northwest corner of Moneo building (light towers on roof)

Pages 142–43: Original William Watkin classical-style south façade with Noguchi sculpture to left

Opposite above left: Central sculpture atrium of Moneo building
Opposite above right: Entry-level lobby of Mies van der Rohe building
Opposite below: Second-level lobby to all galleries of Moneo building
Left: Curving north front designed by Mies van der Rohe

Page 146: Under-street connector between Mies and Moneo buildings (tunnel sculpture by James Turrell)
Page 147 above: Second-floor southwestern gallery
Page 147 below: Second-floor southeast gallery looking northeast

For those who cross its elegant threshold, Mr. Moneo, Peter Marzio, the museum director, and his staff have prepared a stunning surprise: a museum filled with an explosion of overhead natural light and major artworks that have been tucked away in storage for years awaiting a proper installation. Mr. Marzio's request for overhead natural light takes on new meaning upstairs, where the Impressionist and Old Master paintings are being installed. These galleries, which line three sides of the atrium's perimeter, reflect the elegant intimacy of traditional Beaux Arts rooms. In them Mr. Moneo carefully calibrated the flow of light through the roof lanterns, trying to achieve what Mr. Marzio describes as "the frosty glow of a Vermeer." To protect paintings from harmful ultra-violet rays, light strikes an enclosed space hidden in the apex of the ceiling before being deflected downward.
Lisa Germany, *New York Times* (October 31, 1999)

Moneo's almost entirely unfenestrated masonry façades for the Beck Building will be austere. The cladding of Indiana limestone is the same that Mies used, but the strict linearity of Moneo's rectangular box contrasts with the semicircle of the original museum and later wings. Only in its echo of Houston's distant downtown skyline does the roof's mini-village of clustered lanterns acknowledge the building's locale.
Victoria Newhouse, *Towards a New Museum*
(New York: Monacelli Press, 1998)

THE NATIONAL GALLERY OF ART, EAST BUILDING

WASHINGTON, D.C.

I. M. Pei

MUSEUM DIRECTOR'S STATEMENT

The East Building of the National Gallery of Art has delighted the public, scholars, and critics since it was dedicated and opened in June 1978. Its spaces provide eloquent settings for great works of modern art. Its flexible exhibition rooms have been used for nearly two hundred imaginative presentations of the great art of the world, and new exhibitions continue to attract enthusiastic visitors. Its elegant library, offices, and study facilities foster research that enhances our knowledge of art and culture.

- Most impressively, the East Building has taken its place as one of the great public monuments in the nation's capital. Its unusual trapezoidal site at the foot of Capitol Hill presented difficult design challenges for the architect, for the site was relatively small but of the greatest civic and national prominence. The building had to be appropriate for its location on the national Mall and yet was required to meet the museum's programmatic needs. The structure was to be designed in the modern idiom of its time and yet needed to harmonize with John Russell Pope's original West Building and the grand Neoclassical architecture of the Mall and nearby federal triangle. I. M. Pei's great achievement was in balancing these demands, creating a building with lasting majesty and popular appeal.

- The grandeur of the building and its effectiveness for museum functions were the result of a rigorous design process. The building is sensitively linked to its surroundings in every respect. By emphasizing the great angles formed by the Mall and Pennsylvania Avenue, the architect created a building that perfectly integrates the city plan into its own design and is both grandly monumental and open to its urban setting.

- Much of the structure's elegance is due to its extraordinary building materials and careful craftsmanship. The architect insisted that the Tennessee marble quarries that had been used for the original West Building be reopened for the East Building. The stone links the structures and gives the East Building presence and dignity. Its sharp angles and smooth surfaces surprise and delight visitors.

- The East Building was constructed entirely with funds provided by Paul Mellon, Ailsa Mellon Bruce, and the Andrew W. Mellon Foundation. Their generosity and vision, together with the architect's imagination and commitment to excellence, created a grand and ageless structure, now dedicated to the education and enjoyment of the people of the United States.

Earl A. Powell III

ARCHITECT'S STATEMENT

The client requested an expansion facility to complement the existing National Gallery of Art, located on one of the most sensitive sites in the United States. Programmatically, two different buildings were required: a museum to house large traveling exhibitions and provide the infrastructure and ceremonial spaces lacking in the original West Building and a separate office facility to house museum personnel and the newly created Center for Advanced Study in the Visual Arts.

- Three major factors influenced the design: the awkwardly shaped site; the need to respect the original museum and its Neoclassical neighbors while articulating the building in a language of its own time; and the demand for a building monumental enough to anchor its prominent site, but also human in scale. It had to be interesting enough to encourage people to come inside and exciting enough to make them want to return.

- The East Building parallels the converging axes of Pennsylvania Avenue and the Mall. It is subdivided diagonally into two complementary triangles (for the building's two main functions) with a triangular skylighted court unifying the whole. The triangular geometry derived from the site provided the leitmotif for the entire design.

- The skylighted sculpture court provides a large protected space for crowds waiting to see exhibitions and a stage for formal events. It is a hub of public reception, orientation and circulation and also offers relief from museum fatigue. Organized around the court are three flexible exhibition towers designed to present one or more shows simultaneously with the viewing intimacy of a house museum. The Study Center, housed in a smaller triangle adjacent to the public museum, includes a research library, archives, and offices wrapped around a six-story reading room.

- Below ground the two buildings are functionally united by a 154,000-square-foot concourse filled with public and in-house services. Crystal prisms and a 50-foot-long Persian-style water-wall chute, or *chadar,* sculpturally focus the plaza above while bringing natural light into the concourse and animating it with the sight and sound of rushing white water.

- The East Building was designed and executed with a commitment to the highest quality possible. Architectural process, building details and technology were rethought back to their essence in pursuit of that goal. The dedication to excellence was shared not only by the architectural team and the client, but also uniquely by the many contractors and builders involved. The project received forty-five separate Craftsmanship Awards, many times more than the Washington Building Congress had ever conferred on a project.

I. M. Pei, I. M. Pei & Partners Architects

East Building from plaza, showing light-well pyramids and fountain cascade

CRITICS' COMMENTS

For seven years a structure has been rising next to the neoclassical bulk of the National Gallery in Washington: cool, prismatic, with the containment and elegant definition of a quartz crystal. . . . It is the gallery's new East Building, designed by I. M. Pei. . . . It is not an innovative or deliberately spectacular structure, as the still debated Centre Beaubourg in Paris turned out to be. Down to the last miter in its warm Tennessee marble cladding, the East Building is intended to be authoritative, if not exactly authoritarian, statement: balanced, lucid, reflecting the inherently conservative nature of the National Gallery's self-image.
Robert Hughes, *Time* (May 8, 1978)

Superb execution, as one architectural writer put it, is as important to a finished work of art as inspired design; and if Pei's Gallery represents anything, it represents superb execution. It is reassuring that for all its plastic and concrete shoddiness, our time can produce such craftsmanship. . . . Just look at the beauty of the architectural concrete. Generally concrete is an overrated, cheap-looking material. . . . In Pei's building, the concrete is an aggregate of pinkish marble dust poured into forms that are the result of meticulous cabinetwork, made with the care and mitering of parquet floors.
Wolf Von Eckhardt, *Washington Post* (May 7, 1978)

Opposite: South side of building, showing sharp edge corner
Left: East end of central court

Opposite: Cascade Café lit by light pyramids
Above: Central court from east bridge
Left: Two-level Calder gallery

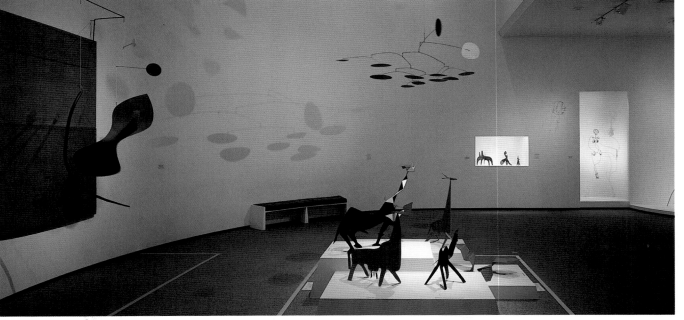

PHOENIX ART MUSEUM PHOENIX, AZ

Alden B. Dow, Tod Williams/Billie Tsien

MUSEUM DIRECTOR'S STATEMENT

The development of Phoenix Art Museum into the largest visual-arts institution in the American Southwest reflects constant commitment from the community it serves. The roots of the museum were planted in 1915, when the art exhibition committee of the Phoenix Women's Club began to acquire art each year and formed the nucleus of a collection. In 1925 the Phoenix Fine Arts Association was formed to foster and promote community art interest and to continue to acquire works of art. The Works Progress Administration (WPA) program to employ artists and begin art galleries around the country created Phoenix Art Center in 1936, the progenitor of Phoenix Art Museum.

▪ In 1948 Phoenix Fine Arts Association was located in a brick house on a property that would later become the 160,000-square-foot museum. Alden B. Dow, a successful Michigan architect who had been a student of Frank Lloyd Wright, designed the museum's first building, which officially opened as Phoenix Art Museum, a private non-profit institution, in 1959.

▪ Over the next forty-four years, the museum has grown to house an important and diverse 17,000-object collection of art that spans traditional, modern, and contemporary art of America, Europe, Latin America, and Asia, as well as fashion design. It enjoys the support of 20,000 members and welcomes hundreds of thousands of visitors each year, including 60,000 children from the Southwest who discover the museum each year through its school tour program.

▪ In 1988 Phoenix voters approved a $20 million bond for expansion and renovation of the museum. Private support supplied the remaining costs of the $25 million project, which was completed in 1996. The building's outstanding classically progressive architecture, designed by award-winning architects Tod Williams/Billie Tsien & Associates of New York City, in association with Lescher and Mahoney/DLR of Phoenix, integrates art and architecture with the Southwestern landscape. The structure provides state-of-the-art gallery systems, uniquely sweeping spaces, and amenities such as a lecture hall, orientation theater, interactive gallery for children, the Art Museum Café and the Museum Store.

▪ Phoenix Art Museum will continue to expand, with new construction expected to begin in late 2004, again as a result of a voter-approved $18 million bond initiative. Tod Williams/Billie Tsien & Associates will again design the expansion as a continuation of the design footprint. The new lobby and additional gallery space will enable the museum to better accommodate the Latin American, modern, and contemporary collections, as well as larger exhibitions and a growing local, national, and international audience.

James K. Ballinger

ARCHITECT'S STATEMENT

This project is an addition to and renovation of an existing civic art museum. Sited directly on Central Avenue, the addition emphasizes this linearity and finds its presence from a sense of grounding and weight. It is a low building with great density.

▪ Two large wings contain the volume of the new exhibition spaces and form the new entrance. The façades slope toward the entrance, imparting a sense of dynamism to the elevation, and ceilings of the interior gallery spaces reveal the slope of the building mass. A bridge, clad in terne-coated stainless steel, connects the two wings at the second floor. The museum visitor passes beneath this threshold to enter a foyer, which serves as a lobby, information center, and connection between the old and new parts of the museum. The addition contains a 350-seat lecture hall and two large, flexible exhibition spaces, a changing exhibits gallery, and the Great Hall, which hosts gala events as well as exhibitions.

▪ The museum is constructed of precast concrete panels with a gray-green calcite aggregate. The color is meant to recall the pale green of the bark of Palo Verde trees and the sagebrush of the desert. The panels form a solid wall that shields the museum from the desert sun. Certain areas are striated to take advantage of the strong shadows. The only glass elements in the front façade are fins of glass that penetrate the concrete and carry a sense of light (but not direct light) into the great hall. The concrete is a quiet plane that catches the moving shadows of the palms and Palo Verdes that are planted along Central Avenue.

▪ Other materials used in the project are simple and common. Blackened concrete, maple, and limestone are used as flooring. Tectum—a wood-fiber product generally found in gymnasiums—is sprayed with metallic paint and used for ceilings and walls. Glass and sandblasted stainless steel are used for railings.

▪ The addition has a tough and somewhat raw clarity. It is a cool oasis, a refuge under the western sun.

Billie Tsien, Tod Wlliams/Billie Tsien & Associates

Entrance, west side

AWARD
- Arizona AIA Merit Award, 1997

CRITICS' COMMENTS

The expansion of the Phoenix Art Museum is a subtle yet unmistakable evocation of motifs of the region, abstracted to the border signification. The building is almost Spanish. Massive precast walls are battered in the load-bearing profile of adobe and topped with a metal cornice. Like roof beams through a mud wall, slabs of green glass penetrate the upper portion of the panels, transmitting not load but light; day in, night out.

Marcel Sorkin, *Architectural Record* (January 1997)

The materials bring the outside in. The celadon-green aggregate of glacier quartz, sand, and mica that skins part of the exterior repeats inside. Walls of pockmarked gray concrete also show up indoors and out. Panels of green glass pierce the exterior walls, appearing on both sides. The cool palette would be depressing in the Northeast; in Phoenix, it's visual air conditioning. The natural materials and organic shapes also remind you that the Phoenix area is home to Frank Lloyd Wright's erstwhile winter headquarters, Taliesin West.

Christine Temin, *Boston Globe* (April 30, 1997)

Opposite: Southwest corridor and gallery
Above left: View down into main southwest gallery
Above right: Northwest corner gallery from second floor viewing window
Left: Upper exhibition space of southwest gallery

Opposite above: East end open sculpture courtyard
and gardens
Opposite below left: Special art interaction room for children
Opposite below right: Northeast-corner galleries
Left: Bridge and entrance plaza

THE PULITZER FOUNDATION FOR THE ARTS ST. LOUIS, MO

Tadao Ando

PRESIDENT'S STATEMENT

My husband and I first heard of Tadao Ando in the late 1980s. The sculptor Richard Serra had just returned from a trip to Japan and told us he had seen the outstanding work of an architect named Tadao Ando. From time to time, other friends mentioned Ando's name to us. James N. Wood had commissioned his first project in the United States, a gallery for Japanese art in the Art Institute of Chicago. When I asked Ellsworth Kelly about Tadao Ando, he replied that he had just recently been sent publications by Ando, who wanted to inaugurate a new gallery he had designed in Japan with an exhibition of Kelly's work. Kelly sent us the material and, after looking at it, my husband and I said with one voice, "This is it. This is the architect we want to create our space." It was an immediate, powerful, aesthetic response.

▪ What began in 1990 as the renovation of a former automobile factory became an entirely new building, which opened as the Pulitzer Foundation for the Arts in October 2001. The Pulitzer Foundation for the Arts is a unique resource for contemplation, enjoyment, and study, which seeks to foster a deeper understanding and appreciation of the art in the context of architecture. Through art, its building, its programs, and collaboration with other arts institutions, these goals are achieved.

▪ Works by Ellsworth Kelly and Richard Serra were commissioned for the Pulitzer Foundation for the Arts, and each artist worked in collaboration with Tadao Ando. These, in addition to a rock settee by Scott Burton and an installation piece, *Atrabiliarios* by Doris Salcedo, comprise the foundation's collection. In the four foundation galleries, installations have remained on view for six months or more. The most recent ones were works by Ellsworth Kelly from St. Louis collections, selected and installed by Kelly, and sculpture and drawings by Richard Serra, also selected and installed by the artist. Docents from the Contemporary Art Partnership (CAP) lead the public programs. CAP is a joint program established by the foundation with the Contemporary Art Museum St. Louis and the St. Louis Art Museum. Other programs, often jointly sponsored with other cultural and educational institutions, have been targeted to various student, scholar, and leadership groups.

Emily Rauh Pulitzer

ARCHITECT'S STATEMENT

I like to think of this project as the creation of "a place of possibility" or "a place of mutual discovery." In other words, I see it as the making of a space to inspire visitors and even expand their consciousness. I wanted to create a stimulating place where works of art are not exhibited as mere specimens but can speak to us as living things.

▪ The project began in 1990 with a letter sent to me by the late Joseph Pulitzer Jr. commissioning a space to house his art collection. At this time, a renewal of part of the decaying city center was being envisioned. The plan focused on a ten-block area in midtown, where a cultural renaissance was already under way. As key figures in that effort, Mr. and Mrs. Pulitzer purchased an old factory, intending to renovate it to house part of their collection of contemporary art. A plan was developed for the site, but the project was postponed during Mr. Pulitzer's terminal illness. Mrs. Pulitzer contacted me in 1993, and we decided to develop an entirely new plan, three years after the project had first been initiated.

▪ Even though the site and the conditions had changed, the concept of creating a place for an inspiring dialogue between art and architecture remained unchanged. During the design, we repeatedly studied the spaces, always imagining the works of art installed in place. What was particularly fortunate about this project was the participation of the artists from the initial stages of the design. Into the spaces I composed with form, material, and light, Ellsworth Kelly and Richard Serra brought their own expression, conceiving a space for art that could exist only there. For me, the exciting collaboration with these artists provided a rare and stimulating opportunity to reconsider the architecture and to rethink what it means to create.

▪ The foundation is a result of more than ten years of great effort by all of the participants. Mrs. Pulitzer, who for many years worked as an art curator, above all constantly demonstrated her passion and professionalism. Her strong will and refusal to compromise propelled the project, and as we moved forward, our affection for the undertaking grew even stronger. It has been a long time since I have had a project that made me long to see it completed and that has given me such delight.

Tadao Ando, Tadao Ando Architect & Associates

Northwest corner

AWARDS
- St. Louis AIA Awards, Honor Award in Architecture, 2002
- Mechanical Contractors Association Award for Outstanding Mechanical Installation (won by Rock Hill Mechanical Corporation), 2002

CRITICS' COMMENTS

A faultless synthesis of art and architecture, it enhances the experience and understanding of both. . . . The insistent horizontality of the linear plan, the discreet distancing of the real world and the minimal, elegant detailing focus all of one's senses on a serene interior of art, light, and form.
Ada Louise Huxtable, *Wall Street Journal*
(March 13, 2002)

Ando is famous for the smoothness and subtlety he demands of concrete surfaces, and the American contractors for this building proved up to the task. The mottled gray-and white-Pulitzer walls are immensely satisfying to see and touch. This quality definitely softens the defensive posture of the outer walls, and helps give them a certain mysterious aura.
Benjamin Forgey, *Washington Post* (October 20, 2001)

Like Frank Lloyd Wright's celebrated Unity Temple in Oak Park, an uncompromising concrete box that shelters a serene, skylit worship space, the Pulitzer building presents a hard-edged face to the world, only revealing itself as the visitor journeys through it.
Blair Kamin, *Chicago Tribune* (October 7, 2001)

Page 164: Office corridor view of reflecting pool and east galleries
Page 165 above: Richard Serra sculpture in courtyard on west side
Page 165 below: East gallery, looking south

Seating stone and reflecting pool

SAN FRANCISCO MUSEUM OF MODERN ART SAN FRANCISCO, CA

Mario Botta

MUSEUM DIRECTOR'S STATEMENT

Since it opened in 1995 on the occasion of the museum's sixtieth anniversary, the San Francisco Museum of Modern Art has become almost as much of an attraction for visitors as the art it showcases. The renowned Swiss architect Mario Botta designed the structure. It was his first museum and first project in the United States.

• The opening of the new building signaled a transformation for SFMOMA as an institution and for the South of Market neighborhood in which it is located. Formerly quartered in the War Memorial Veterans Building—a much smaller and older facility that was never intended to be a museum—SFMOMA found itself back on the map after its relocation. Gallery space was doubled (to 50,000 square feet), and state-of-the-art facilities were allocated for education, new-media presentations, lectures, and art conservation and storage. But most important, the new museum building embodies the aesthetic values of the institution it houses. Whereas the old building was a Beaux-Arts homage to the architecture of the past, Botta's creation is a work of modern art. Its clean but complex geometric forms, crowned with a distinctive oculus, make it a widely recognizable landmark. It attracts more than six hundred thousand visitors every year, and Bay Area residents repeatedly name it their favorite local museum—a distinction that modern-art museums in other cities almost never enjoy.

• From a visitor's perspective, the structure's most impressive feature is its five-story entrance atrium, topped by an enormous turret and slanted skylight. Leading off from the atrium are the café, store, theater, special-events rooms, and other amenities. A suspended footbridge on the fifth floor provides a dramatic view of the atrium from above. Inside the galleries, rooms containing paintings and sculpture enjoy a mixture of natural and artificial light, while smaller galleries devoted to light-sensitive works on paper are designed without skylights. Other spaces are specially configured to showcase touring exhibitions or digital and multimedia installations. There is even a small outdoor sculpture terrace.

• As SFMOMA has settled into its new home, one of its most important priorities has been to provide the public with more (and more meaningful) access to the permanent collection of modern and contemporary art. Part of its staff was recently moved out of the main building so that 7,000 square feet of office space could be converted into the Koret Visitor Education Center. This facility is not hidden in the basement, like most museum education centers, but is immediately adjacent to the galleries and includes ample room for classes, art activities, film screenings, and computer kiosks where visitors of all ages can learn more about the art they have just encountered.

Neal Benezra

ARCHITECT'S STATEMENT

The typology of any building is determined by two conditions—the function it must carry out and the site where it must rise. In the case of the San Francisco Museum of Modern Art, the building's primary function is to exhibit contemporary works of art that require large spaces. For this reason, I have envisioned a design characterized by peripheral galleries that are principally illuminated by skylights.

• The character of the site is also critical. The fact that this museum will be located in the center of the city, while most recent museum projects have been set in less dense surroundings, makes it unique. I therefore created a large open area, represented by a central court and surrounded by the exhibition spaces. On a lot of only 65,000 square feet, the building's program calls for about 225,000 square feet.

• Natural light is a specific element tied to a geographic location. I like the thought that the art on display will be viewed through the "real" light of the city. With filters and veils, you can control and modulate light through skylights, thereby offering optimum conditions while also leaving the walls completely available as expository surfaces.

• I think a relationship based on dialogue is imperative between the architecture and the works of art. The works of art require optimal spaces to be completely enjoyed and, likewise, the gallery spaces need the works of art in order to acquire their full dimensions. In museums, the real challenge is to discover that perfect balance where the architecture and art enrich one another.

• Besides the ground floor, which is reserved for all public spaces—café, event space, bookstore, auditorium, and educational facilities—the museum's interior offers three areas. The atrium, the true heart of the building, is the center of spatial gravity for the entire museum, the point from which visitors have access to the museum's various functions and levels. It is an architectonically drawn space, with the light from above serving as a type of cornice for the museum visitor. The galleries, on the upper levels, offer a subdued and calm architectural space devoted to the works of art. The back area, which is reserved for offices and services, provides functional spaces that aim to offer the maximum amount of natural light to the working areas.

Mario Botta

Façade, from public plaza across street

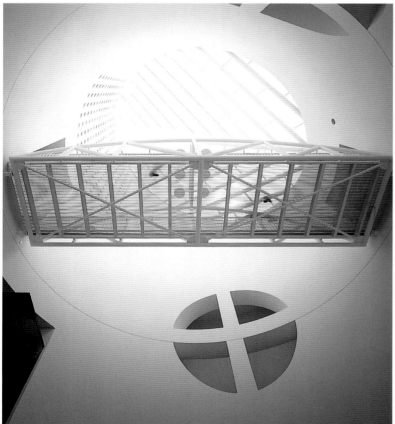

AWARDS
- American Institute of Architects (California) Merit Award for Excellence in Design, 1995
- Marble Architectural Award America of Carrara (Italy), 1997

CRITICS' COMMENTS

Extraordinary . . . majestic . . . at times technically beyond praise . . . one of the best museum buildings of our time."
Allan Temko, *San Francisco Focus* (January 1995)

The design partly recalls Wright's for the Guggenheim, and, a little, Louis Kahn's for the Yale Center for British Art. But it also alludes to Italy; people at the museum talk a lot about Mr. Botta's lobby being like a piazza, his stairwell a campanile. Like a piazza, the lobby is supposed to be a gathering place, its store and café and theater a magnet to draw visitors, even those who don't want to see art.
- Mr. Botta's galleries are the strength of the new San Francisco Museum of Modern Art. The transitions from them to the round stairwell make for awkward spaces. . . . But the rooms themselves are plain, practical, and, thanks to the step-backs, many can be skylighted. Indeed, Mr. Botta's handling of light in the galleries is almost as fine as Kahn's at the Kimbell Art Museum in Fort Worth, which is saying a lot.
Michael Kimmelman, *New York Times*
(January 24, 1995)

Opposite above: Northwest-corner galleries on third floor
Opposite below left: Upper bridge in light shaft used to access top galleries by stairs
Opposite below right: View of central space from north-side balcony
Left: Main entrance lobby and central light shaft/atrium

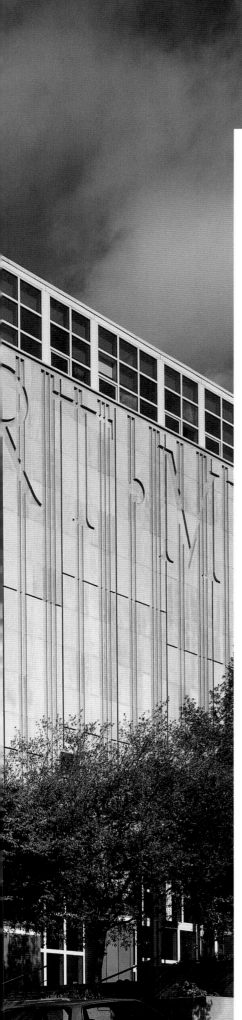

SEATTLE ART MUSEUM

Robert Venturi/Denise Scott Brown

MUSEUM DIRECTOR'S STATEMENT

For decades, the Seattle Art Museum (SAM) has collected and exhibited works of art that span across cultures and time. Founded in 1933 by Dr. Richard Fuller in Seattle's Volunteer Park, the museum's outstanding permanent collection includes more than 23,000 fine works. The collection is particularly strong in six areas: Asian, African, Northwest Coast Native American, modern art, European painting, and decorative arts. Their range and depth are unmatched in the region.

- The museum outgrew its original home designed in 1933 by Carl Gould in Volunteer Park and expanded into the heart of downtown Seattle in 1991. SAM's leaders sought out world-renowned architect Robert Venturi of Venturi Scott Brown & Associates, Inc., to design a new building for the museum. The recipient of numerous fellowships and honorary degrees, Venturi is known for work that rebels against the "less is more" theory.

- On December 5, 1991, the new downtown Seattle Art Museum opened its doors to the public, and the press called it an architectural gem. To establish it as a presence amid the surrounding skyscrapers, Venturi emphasized the grand-scale elegance of its public spaces, primarily the ground-level lobby and second-floor entryway into the galleries. With its large windows, alternating pediments and arches, terraced staircase, and sensuous combination of granites, marbles, and colored terra-cotta, the first two floors announced the building itself as a work of art without upstaging the galleries. In its first fiscal year, the museum attracted 9,500 new members, and the total membership is currently just under 30,000. Attendance often exceeds 500,000 visitors each year.

- In 1994 the original Gould building was renovated and became the Seattle Asian Art Museum, housing a superb collection of Asian art and traveling exhibitions of Asian art. As we enter our eighth decade, the Seattle Art Museum is embarking on two major projects. First, we are planning an expansion of the downtown museum, which is being designed by Brad Cloepfil of Allied Works Architecture of Portland, Oregon. The expansion will provide the museum with much needed gallery space, a new lobby, and public areas for our visitors, as well as such amenities as an expanded store and restaurant. We are also creating the Olympic Sculpture Park, an eight-and-a-half-acre park on Seattle's waterfront featuring dynamic art and views of the Puget Sound, Olympic Mountains, and the city's skyline. These projects will reinforce artistic excellence and our strong commitment to the community, benefiting the region culturally and economically.

Mimi Gates

ARCHITECTS' STATEMENT

This building is itself a work of art, yet one that does not upstage the art inside but serves instead as a background. It conforms not to the current trend of the museum as expressionistic, dramatic pavilions, but to an older tradition, the adapted palaces and grand museums of the nineteenth century and the original Museum of Modern Art in New York, the museum as generic loft.

- Given its context downtown in an American city, within a grid plan, and sited along a street like any other building, the museum building must derive its civic quality not because of its special location (at the end of a boulevard for instance), but through its combinations of scales—both large and small—and its iconographic ornament. Although a relatively small building (153,000 square feet), the Seattle Art Museum holds its own among the larger buildings around it because of these qualities.

- The play of small- and large-scale elements helps make the building friendly from the outside, despite its overall lack of windows, and this sense is enhanced at eye level through the building's openness and its lyrical rhythms, color, and ornament.

- The rectangular plan of the loft is broken at the southwest, where the corner is rounded to generate exterior civic space and accommodate the main entrance and a civic sculptural figure, making the museum both civic and civil.

- Civic scale penetrates the interior by means of the grand stair, which is parallel to and visible from the sidewalk stair outside and makes the building feel open and accessible.

- A complex program for a modern museum must serve a heterogeneous community, house educational, administrative, and commercial-café activities, and provide support space for services, storage, and conservation, as well as the primary space for the exhibition of art. All of these can be accommodated within the generic loft system promoted by this design. The flexibility of the loft space allows the museum's various and growing collections to be displayed within the varying cultural and physical contexts appropriate to particular art works and to diverse audiences, and it allows evolving changes among the service-support programs.

- Variations in structural bay sizes provide a three-zone organization on all levels of the building. The longer spans on the north side house bigger, more flowing sequences of spaces. Bays along the south façade suit installations requiring smaller spaces. The intermediate zone accommodates services and circulation, and at each end are windows, where visitors can orient themselves to the outside and experience natural light. Vistas across the parallel series of zones provide opportunities for cross-cultural comparisons and visual contrasts.

Robert Venturi/Denise Scott Brown, Venturi Scott Brown & Associates, Inc.

Southwest-corner entrance

CRITICS' COMMENTS

What is surprising is the substantiality and craftsmanship of the fluted limestone exterior. All the building materials—including granite, reddish sandstone, bluestone, and polychromed terra-cotta—give the museum a monumental weight and texture. The detailing, elegant if quixotic, adds a level of refinement. Even the billboardlike lettering of the museum's name is carved in stone. All in all, the contradiction between solid materials and abstractly referential patterns, between impeccable details and chunky form, emphatically delivers the message of "both-and" principle governing much of the architecture of Robert Venturi and Denise Scott Brown.
Suzanne Stephens, *Architecture* (1992)

The shift to downtown itself is a clear symbol of the city's aspirations for this institution. This building is not only in downtown, it is of downtown. It is no icon, no shimmering piece of sculpture set on a pedestal; the museum takes its cues from both the architecture and the topography around it, calling out to the old brick and terra-cotta buildings nearby, and letting the hill inspire its major architectural gesture, a vast, sprawling staircase from the main entrance at the lower level to the gallery spaces above.
Paul Goldberger, *New York Times* (February 16, 1992)

The stairway is functionless in the literal sense, but extremely important to the greater functioning of the building. It is where its essence resides. It serves as a stage on which the citizens of Seattle can come to see and be seen. The museum restaurant spills onto it like a sidewalk café.
David Bonetti, *San Francisco Examiner* (February 20, 1992)

Opposite: Looking up grand stairway from entrance lobby
Left: African art gallery
Below left: South façade ornamentation

UNIVERSITY OF WYOMING ART MUSEUM LARAMIE, WY

Antoine Predock

MUSEUM DIRECTOR'S STATEMENT

Wyoming is a state of vast geographic expanses, extreme weather, and a population of less than 500,000. The University of Wyoming is the state's only four-year institution of higher education, and the University of Wyoming Art Museum is the only institution in the state to present art of all periods from the region, nation, and the world. An educational institution with a mission to "collect, preserve, exhibit, and interpret a broad spectrum of visual arts of the highest quality and of national importance for this and future generations," the art museum has a collection that includes nearly 7,000 paintings, works on paper, sculpture, crafts, photography, and ethnographic material from cultures around the globe. Collecting areas include modern and contemporary art, American and European art, photography, and arts of the Americas, Africa, Easter Island, and Southeastern Asia.

- Realizing that the students at the university and the people of Wyoming needed to experience original work in order that art be appropriately taught and appreciated, Professor James Boyle, a studio artist and head of the art department, began to collect art for the university in the 1960s. The art museum was established in 1972, when it opened in the Fine Arts Building, a then-new facility that also housed the departments of art, music, theater, and dance.

- Within fifteen years, a collection of nearly 5,000 objects had been acquired, and the need for a controlled environment, increased storage areas and galleries, additional staff, and expanded support areas became paramount. In 1986 the University of Wyoming launched its Centennial Campaign, the centerpiece of which was a new facility for the art museum and the American Heritage Center, which houses the university's archives. Through a design competition, the University of Wyoming trustees selected Antoine Predock as the architect of the Centennial Complex.

- In 1993 the art museum opened in the state-of-the-art Centennial Complex, a facility that provides 12,000 square feet of exhibition space, a 700-square-foot art studio for education programs, and 5,100 square feet for collection storage. The exhibition program mirrors the collecting areas and features contemporary art, interdisciplinary programs on subjects of the American West, and culturally diverse exhibitions from all periods.

Susan B. Moldenhauer

ARCHITECT'S STATEMENT

In the landscape in the American West, a work of architecture confronts daunting expanses of land and geologic formations. It is very difficult to perceive the scale of natural features and to create an impact on them with a building. The distant Snowy Range and the nearer Laramie Range frame the site for the American Heritage Center and Art Museum, each highlighted by a single peak. The axis of the project is aligned with these two summits—Medicine Bow Peak and Pilot's Knob.

- In contrast to buildings in towns of the Old West, which adopted classical pediments to assert their presence, the American Heritage Center and Art Museum, completed in 1993, is a consciously monumental landscape abstraction that represents a symbol for future campus growth to the northeast, and a statement of the powerful spirit of Wyoming. Two discrete forms—an archival mountain and a clustered village—give separate identity to each facility and celebrate hearth, visitor research areas, lobby, permanent and traveling galleries. These forms rest on a landscape-integrated base containing work and storage area with internal organization of the complex defined by nodes of fire and light.

- Native Americans, early trappers, and Oregon Trail emigrants relied on organized gatherings to provide a sense of community in a landscape that resists settlement. The building presents a cultural nexus for intellectual and social gathering, the original rendezvous made permanent.

Antoine Predock

East end of museum from upper level, showing outdoor sculpture court

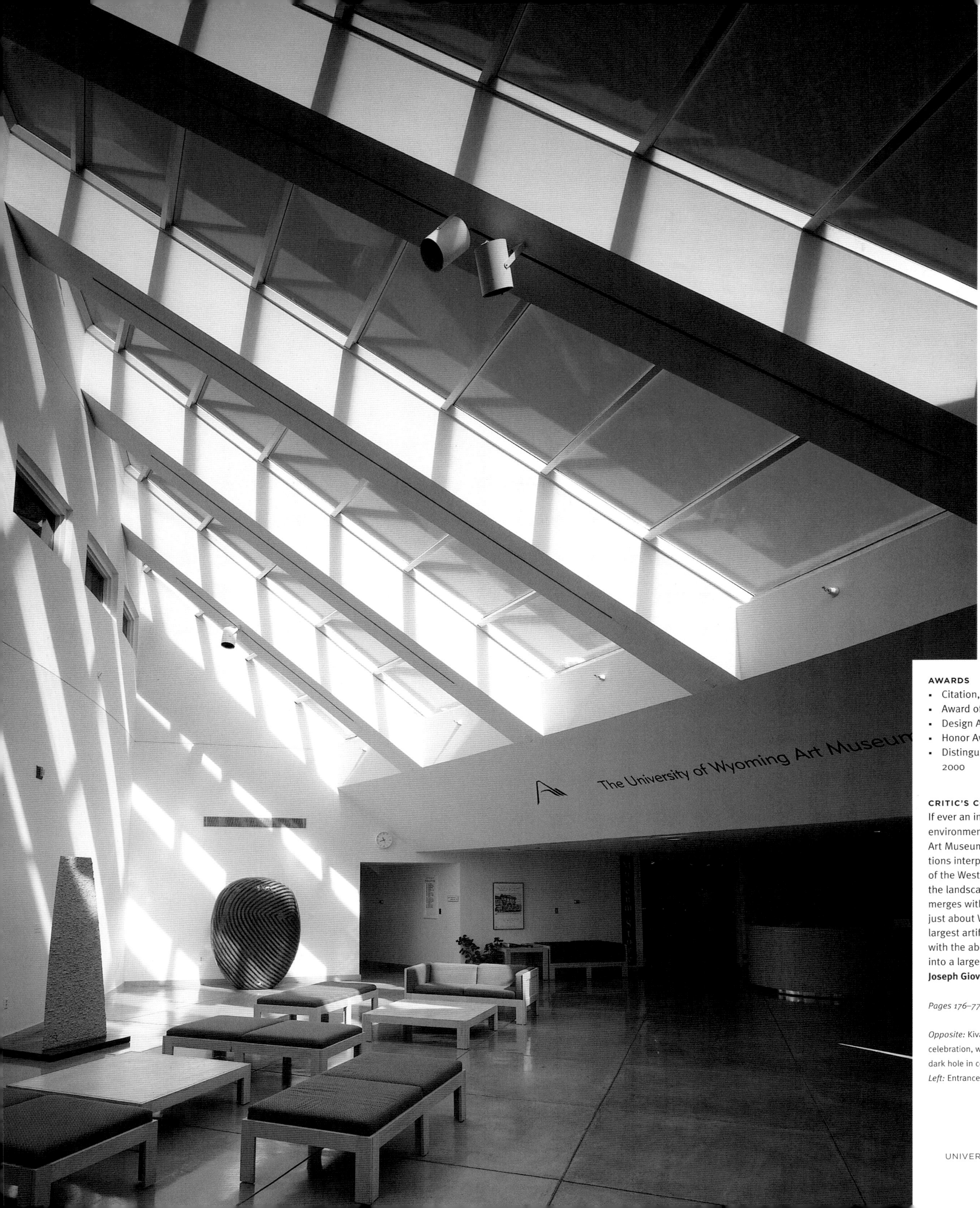

The University of Wyoming Art Museum

AWARDS

- Citation, Progressive Architecture, 1990
- Award of Excellence, AIA New Mexico Design, 1993
- Design Award, Concrete Masonry Award, 1994
- Honor Award, AIA Western Mountain Region, 1995
- Distinguished Award of Honor, AIA International, 2000

CRITIC'S COMMENT

If ever an institutional program complemented its environment, it is the American Heritage Center and Art Museum, largely because so much of both collections interpret and document the history and culture of the West. Predock's building, which intensifies the landscape and Indian associations, seamlessly merges with them, becoming of Wyoming rather than just about Wyoming and the West. The building is the largest artifact in the collection, but a living artifact with the ability to de-accession itself and dissolve into a larger ethos.
Joseph Giovannini, *Architecture* (December 1993)

Pages 176–77: Southwest view of museum

Opposite: Kiva-inspired round gallery (site of summer-solstice celebration, where high-noon shaft of light comes through dark hole in ceiling and hits mark in center of room
Left: Entrance lobby

YALE CENTER FOR BRITISH ART
NEW HAVEN, CT

Louis I. Kahn

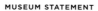

MUSEUM STATEMENT

Thanks to the extraordinary generosity of Paul Mellon, class of 1929, Yale University boasts the most comprehensive collection of British art outside the United Kingdom, as well as the landmark building by Louis I. Kahn in which it is housed. Located directly across Chapel Street from the Yale University Art Gallery (1951–53), Kahn's first major commission, the Yale Center for British Art, is the architect's final building. From the entrance portico, the visitor is drawn into the first of two skylighted interior courtyards that reflect the center's dual mission, as both a public museum and a research center.

- Kahn's choice of natural materials (white oak, linen, and travertine) and his insistence on the use of natural light (which is filtered through skylights on the fourth floor and enters through side windows throughout the building) create interior spaces that are both elegant and subdued. The public galleries are domestic in scale and provide ideal conditions in which to view works of art. Just as vistas through the galleries and across the interior courtyards orient visitors inside the building, views through the windows to the street place the Yale Center within the university's arts district and the city of New Haven. In addition, the ever-changing light serves as a subtle reminder of the time of day and the season of the year.

- The placement of offices, classrooms, a 200-seat lecture hall, a reference library and study room (where works on paper can be examined), and a conservation laboratory contiguous to the public spaces on each floor, encourages exchange among different users of the building.

- While the collections and staff have grown considerably, and programming has become more extensive over the course of the past three decades, the Yale Center for British Art has adapted to the increased demands and continues to serve the needs of students and scholars, staff and members of the public alike. Major capital projects that have been undertaken to date include replacement of the side windows, renovation of the roof, refurbishment of the galleries, and the creation of a room in honor of Paul Mellon, as well as retrofits of art-storage areas and library stacks in order to accommodate growing collections.

- An international team of scholars, architects, and museum professionals was recently appointed to explore the building's history, to develop a building-conservation plan, and to address future needs of what many consider Yale's most distinguished modern building.

Constance Clement, Deputy Director

ARCHITECT'S STATEMENT

Louis Kahn died before the museum was completed. What follows is an excerpt from The Architecture of the Yale Center for British Art (1977) *by founding museum director Jules David Prown, who played a central role in the selection of the architect, the development of the program, and negotiations between the donor, the university, and the architect.*

- The center . . . is a four-story steel and glass building on a double-court plan, with commercial shops at street level along Chapel and High Streets. Developed on a module of twenty-foot square bays, the rectangular building extends for ten bays along Chapel Street and six bays in depth.

- The façade of the center reflects Kahn's fondness for the juxtaposition of materials closely matched in color and texture. Once, during the long design process, Kahn responded to the client's impatient query to what the building would look like with the comment, "On a grey day it will look like a moth; on a sunny day like a butterfly." The image of the moth refers to the closely matched appearance of the dull steel and glass on a grey day. . . .

- I had reservations . . . about the use of steel on the façade, which I feared would be cold and impersonal. I told Kahn I did not much like metal buildings, and asked him if he had ever seen a metal-clad building that pleased him. "No," he said. "But you like stainless steel for this building?" "Yes!" Despite his lack of enthusiasm for metal as generally applied architecturally as a surface material, he responded to the esthetic as well as structural qualities of certain metals (he liked metal mechanical elements to be exposed), and felt that the special working relationship of glass and steel for light admission, and the pleasing visual effect of these closely matched materials with each other and with the structural concrete made the choice appropriate for the center.

- More important than the British Art Center's historical role as Kahn's last building is its own architectural distinction. With its regular features and clear articulation of structure, the center possesses a classical serenity. But like classical architecture at its best, it projects an individual presence. Although the building is strong, it achieves its distinction by modest and subtle means—perfect proportions, sensitively matched materials, and honest expression of structure. It is independent, yet sympathetic to its varied architectural neighbors. It is respectful of the urban character of its setting, with shops bordering the sidewalk at ground level and an open entrance portico at the corner which allows the street to reach into the building. From the exterior, glimpses through the windows, the interruption of the stainless steel drips and concrete beams on three sides, and the splash of daylight seen in a courtyard beyond the glass entrance doors suggest the magic of the interior spaces.

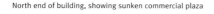
North end of building, showing sunken commercial plaza

CRITICS' COMMENTS

The Yale Center, like much recent architecture of all building types and styles, rejected neutral, placeless spaces in favor of the genius loci and specificity. It took a stand in favor of relating interiors to nature and the city through use of ample, framed openings, the layering of space, natural materials, controlled daylight, courtyards, a Beaux-Arts plan with distinct rooms, even intimate residential galleries. And it influenced many museums since.
Andrea Oppenheimer Dean, *Architecture*
(January 1986)

Louis I. Kahn's Yale Center for British Art was an unexpected culmination of his career. Two decades earlier, Kahn had set out to free himself from the volumetric envelope of Mies van der Rohe's design. . . . But in the British Art Center, effectively his last constructed building, he not only went straight back to the volume and bay system of Mies but also brought glass forward to operate at its maximum capacity for visual magic in translucency and reflection. . . . He produced a perfect box, its long side pressed flat to the street and stretched along it.
Vincent Scully, *Architectural Record* (June 1977)

Opposite above: View into entrance atrium, showing galleries wrapped around open space
Opposite below: Cylindrical stairwell
Left: Main-entrance atrium lobby

Fourth-floor gallery from exit of stairwell

Opposite: Northwest view of Great Gallery

Above: Fourth floor, southeast-corner painting galleries

WORKS
IN
PROGRESS

AKRON ART MUSEUM AKRON, OH

Coop Himmelb(l)au

MUSEUM DIRECTOR'S STATEMENT

Beginning with its first exhibitions in 1922, the Akron Art Museum has embraced the visual arts in all forms, from painting and sculpture to commercial design and photography. In the 1970s, the museum refocused its exhibitions and collections to concentrate solely on visual art produced since 1850. The collection of more than 3,000 objects is especially strong in twentieth-century photography, contemporary sculpture, and post-modern painting. It also includes work by American Impressionists and important regional artists.

• The new museum will be built directly adjacent to the existing facility, an 1899 brick post office inspired by the Florentine Renaissance and converted into a museum in 1980. The addition will be twice the size of the existing building and will contain 22,000 square feet of flexible galleries and extensive new spaces for public education and leisure, including an auditorium, classrooms, a children's gallery, a bookstore, a café, and a dramatic, soaring lobby. Key program requirements include an improved system for deliveries and the reorientation of the main entrance to face a new parking deck built by the city of Akron across the street from the museum. Phase I will result in 65,000 square feet of enclosed space, with an anticipated opening in summer 2006. Phase II will create a 20,000-square-foot outdoor sculpture courtyard and reconfigure part of the interior of the 1899 building.

• The key challenge of the commission is contradictory: preserve the existing nineteenth-century landmark but link it to a dynamic new structure consonant with the museum's reputation for innovation. The selection process began with a review of 121 firms by a panel of architects. Thirty firms were then asked to submit design proposals. Three superb finalists, none of whom had built in Ohio, were chosen and visited by a selection committee: Snøhetta (Oslo); UNstudio van Berkel and Bos (Amsterdam); and Coop Himmelb(l)au (Vienna). Each received an honorarium and travel expenses and examined the building site before producing models and plans.

• Coop Himmelb(l)au's scheme was chosen for its daring compression of the two buildings into one, whereas the other proposals created two separate structures. Himmelb(l)au leaves three façades of the 1899 building untouched but in a radical gesture cuts open the rear façade to link it to the new glass lobby. Improbably, unity rather than imitation results from a contrast of forms and materials. The startling embrace of old and new is heralded outside by a soaring roof cantilevered above the existing building and out over the city's major artery. In a provocative symbolic gesture, the crystalline glass lobby opposes the metal box of the enclosed galleries suspended above. We are reminded that museums are a balancing act: public, populist, and open but also private, authoritative, and protective.

Mitchell Kahan

ARCHITECT'S STATEMENT

The museum of the twenty-first century is changing its role. Far from being the repository of accumulated cultural knowledge and production or a filtered space of contact with Knowledge, the museum is shedding its "cathedral" role and migrating toward that of an Urban Event Space. As society and production become more networked, the role of the museum must change. It can no longer be involved with the maintenance of a cultural elite and the preservation of high culture over low. Rather, in a contemporary cultural environment, the museum is an event space, a destination, and a place in the city where one can simultaneously have contact with art, commerce, and the community.

• The new Akron Art Museum fills this role, blending into the fabric of the city and allowing for multiple types of approaches. One can enter the museum to come into contact with art, to linger in the grand lobby and meet others, to have lunch in the café, browse the bookstore, or any combination of these. The traditional filters that mediate one's progress into the sanctuaries of art have been replaced by an open envelope that allows for multiple types and speeds of progress through the structure.

• Spatially, the Akron Art Museum is composed of three main elements. The windowless gallery space cantilevers over the grand lobby and creates visual tension on South High Street. Inside it is flexible and reconfigurable, allowing for the display of wide variations of exhibits. The crystal houses the grand lobby and becomes a public icon of openness for the city. It creates a space of leisure, where one can be in the museum and in the city simultaneously. It is a nexus, connecting the floating galleries with street life and commercial functions. It is at once a space of activity and contemplation.

• The Roof Cloud floats over the other elements of the museum, blurring the envelope and suggesting the extension of the museum into the city. The tips of the "wings" provide another level of urban presence, one that provides visual access to the museum from a distance, announcing the museum as an integral part of the new city.

• The Akron Art Museum will become a center of activity for the city, a place of learning, a gathering place, and a major event space. Its very openness will propose new types of cultural existence for the city and its people. Its accessibility will insure that it becomes a new urban focus, extending the museum into the very fabric of the city.

Thomas Wiscombe, Coop Himmelb(l)au

Renderings of addition by Coop Hiimelb(l)au (courtesy of the Akron Art Museum)

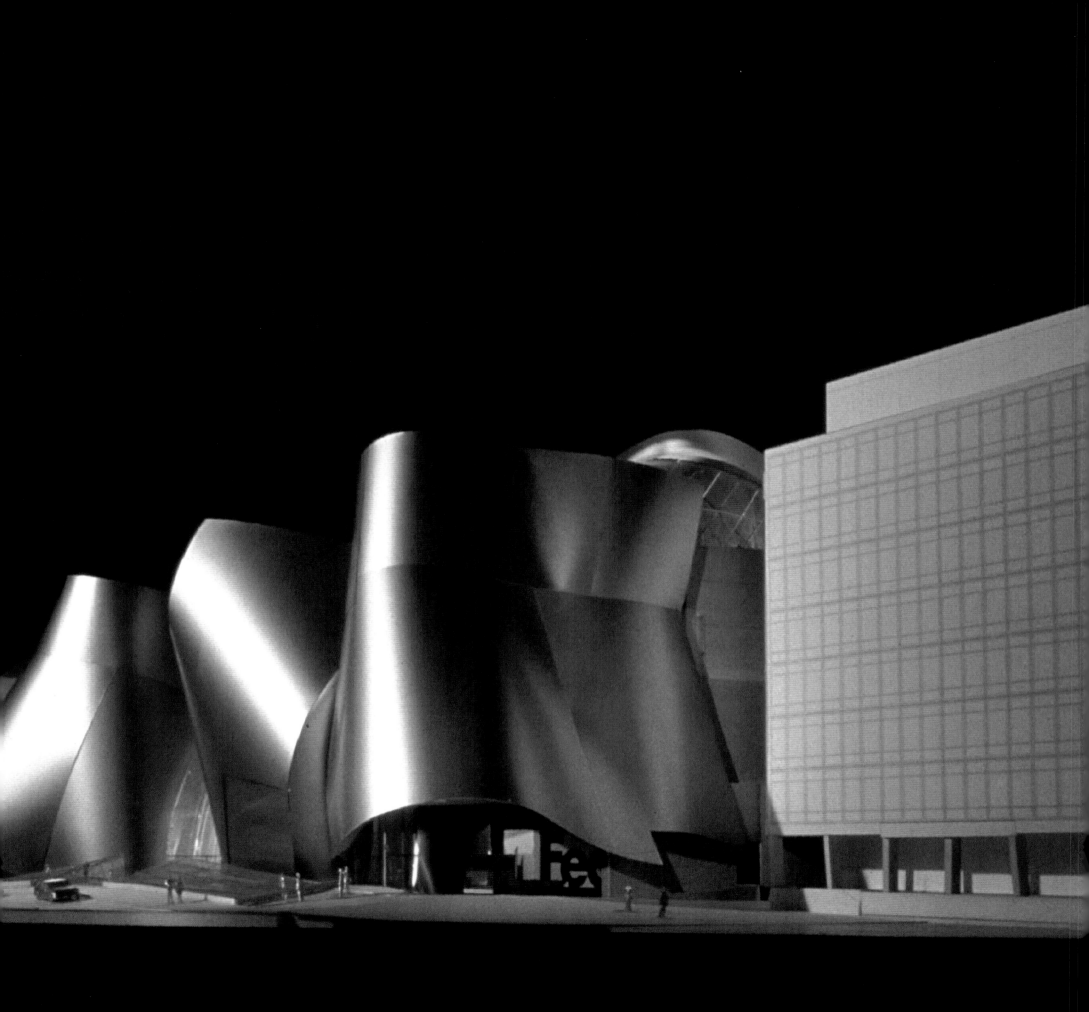

THE CORCORAN GALLERY OF ART

Ernest Flagg, Charles Platt, Frank O. Gehry

MUSEUM DIRECTOR'S STATEMENT

The Corcoran Gallery of Art was founded in 1869 to provide a museum "dedicated to art and used solely for the purpose of encouraging American genius." With a rich history of contributing to the cultural life of Washington, D.C., the Corcoran is a progressive museum and college responsive to the evolving needs of its community, the nation, and the international art world.

▪ Over the past five years, the Corcoran has experienced unprecedented growth. Museum membership has tripled; three thousand objects have been added to the collection, and enrollment to the Corcoran College of Art + Design has increased by 60 percent. To meet the needs of an astoundingly diverse institution, the Corcoran has commissioned the celebrated architect Frank O. Gehry to renovate and expand the Corcoran complex, reinforcing the close partnership between the museum and the college. Highlights include the construction of a new wing; reconfiguring and recapturing significant space in the historic building; and adding approximately 140,000 square feet of flexible space for classrooms, galleries, a restaurant, a shop, and offices. Restoration of the historic building will also improve the existing facilities for the display, conservation, and storage of art work. In addition to an important collection of American paintings and the Clark Collection of nineteenth-century European artists, the Corcoran boasts extensive contemporary art holdings, and the Corcoran Biennials cultivate the work of emerging artists.

▪ The Corcoran recognizes its obligation to commission a building that conceptually, visually, and technically embodies the best architectural ideas of the time. After reviewing qualifications and projects of more than two hundred architectural firms, the Corcoran's architecture-selection committee and trustees chose three distinguished finalists: Santiago Calatrava, Frank O. Gehry, and Daniel Libeskind. In the end, Mr. Gehry's stunning originality, coupled with his deep respect for the Corcoran's historic buildings (by Ernest Flagg and Charles Platt), his meticulous study of our program, and his ability to combine his progressive vision with our practical needs, carried the day.

▪ By offering a spectacular new piece of contemporary architecture while restoring a historic building to its original use, the new Corcoran Gallery of Art will stand as a symbol of the creativity and power of art for generations to come. The Corcoran views its new building program as an act of civic responsibility: a gift to future Americans and visitors from around the world who come here to celebrate, at their source, the freedoms and creative imagination that have so profoundly distinguished our country.

David C. Levy

ARCHITECT'S STATEMENT

I am deeply honored to have been selected for this unusually challenging project. At the outset, I understood that the process of design and the give-and-take with Corcoran president and director David C. Levy, chairman of the board Ronald Abramson, and the Corcoran team could provoke something entirely new for me. The special relationship between the Corcoran's museum and college provides opportunities that reflect my own interests and background.

▪ One of the main goals of the project is to harmonize old and new, respecting the integrity of the original Beaux-Arts building designed by Ernest Flagg while leading the Corcoran architecturally into the twenty-first century. Essentially an urban infill project, the design compositionally unifies the city block by deriving the language for the response from Ernest Flagg's hemicycle on the corner of New York Avenue and 17th Street. The curve of the Hemicycle Gallery was used to generate the concept for three forms along New York Avenue, reflecting the same size, scale, and massing of the existing structure. Shapes angled upward tie the height of the Flagg building to the height of the United Unions building. The majority of the addition is not visible from the Seventeenth Street façade, allowing the character of the historic façade to retain its primary impact while also providing glimpses of the addition from E Street and Seventeenth Street.

▪ A light-filled central atrium is a most dynamic aspect of the design. It reinforces the entrance and axis of Flagg's building and unifies all subsequent additions. Significantly, the atrium realizes Flagg's original vision of a loop of galleries ringing a central space. By linking the museum to the college, the atrium also enacts the institutional identity of the Corcoran. The college is placed in an area below grade linking horizontally with galleries above. This vaulted space calls for two sweeping skylights that cast natural light into studios, dramatize the college's own centering space and announce its equal presence at the new museum entrance. All of the college's spaces will be organized around this atrium to create a vibrant and welcoming hub where students and faculty can meet and exchange ideas.

Frank O. Gehry, Frank O. Gehry & Associates

Renderings of addition and remodeling by Frank O. Gehry (courtesy of The Corcoran Gallery of Art)

DENVER ART MUSEUM

Gio Ponti, Daniel Libeskind

Founded in 1893 as the Denver Artist's Club, the Denver Art Museum did not have a permanent address until more than seventy-five years later. In 1971, the museum moved into its current home, a seven-story, two-tower, 210,000-square-foot building designed by Italian architect Gio Ponti and Denver-based James Sudler Associates. Covered in more than one million glass tiles, the castlelike structure was—and remains today—an iconic piece of architecture as well as being Gio Ponti's only completed building in North America. Aside from creating much-needed space for the presentation of our comprehensive collections of art, this building allowed for more accurate control of temperature and humidity within the galleries. With its nontraditional design, the building also exemplified the museum's innovative and bold attitude toward the display and interpretation of artwork.

- The explosive rise in population and a consistently growing appetite for art and culture throughout Denver and the surrounding region led to increases in the museum's attendance, membership, programs, and collections. This growth paved the way for the museum's most ambitious expansion project since the completion of the Ponti-designed building in 1971. In November 1999, Denver voters overwhelmingly approved a bond initiative to allocate $62.5 million for an expansion building. Less than a year later, after reviewing proposals from more than forty architects, the museum announced that architect Daniel Libeskind had been selected to lead the project.

- Libeskind envisioned a structure unlike any other in the world, but one that would complement the existing architecture, a connection for the surrounding neighborhoods and a pillar for the city of Denver. Its jagged shape, which has been compared to a crystal, an origami swan, and a metallic flower, was inspired by the area's rugged landscape. Clad in shining titanium, the 146,000-square-foot Frederic C. Hamilton Building will feature a dramatic four-story atrium and gallery spaces that will allow us for the first time to dedicate permanent space to our collections of modern and contemporary art, African art, and Oceanic art. With room to accommodate as many as three major special exhibitions at a time, the museum will be able to welcome the world's most prestigious traveling shows. The building will also contain new spaces for educational programs, including the museum's acclaimed offerings for families and children.

Lewis I. Sharp

The new building for the Denver Art Museum will be an icon whose character and form will attract a wide public to the museum complex. The new building is a nexus tying together downtown and civic center, forming a strong connection to the Golden Triangle neighborhood to the south. The nexus is conceived in close connection with the function and aesthetic of the existing museum, as well as the entire Civic Center and the public library. The project is not designed as a stand-alone building but as part of a composition of public spaces, monuments, and gateways in this developing part of the city, contributing to the synergy amongst neighbors large and intimate.

- The materials for the building will be those closely relating to the existing context (local stone) as well as innovative new materials (titanium), which together will form spaces that connect local Denver tradition to the twenty-first century.

- The amazing vitality and growth of Denver, from its foundation to the present, inspires the form of new museum. Coupled with the magnificent topography with its breathtaking views of the sky and the Rocky Mountains, the dialogue between the boldness of construction and the romanticism of the landscape create a unique place in the world. The bold and forward-looking engagement of the public in forging its own cultural, urban, and spirited destiny is something that would strike anyone upon touching the soil of Colorado.

- One of the challenges of building the Denver Art Museum is to work closely with and respond to the extraordinary range of transformations in light, coloration, atmospheric effects, and temperature and weather conditions unique to this city. I insist these are to be integrated not only functionally and physically, but also culturally and experientially for the benefit of the visitors' experience. The conjunction of the contemporary art experience with the uniqueness of the local conditions will form part of the decisions regarding materials, form, and space.

- The new building is not based on an idea of style or the rehashing of ready-made ideas or external shapes, because its architecture does not separate the inside from the outside or provide a pretty façade behind which a typical experience exists. Rather, this architecture has an organic connection to the public at large and to those aspects of experience that are also intellectual, emotional, and sensual. The integration of these dimensions for the enjoyment and edification of the public is achieved in a building that respects the handcrafted nature of architecture and its immediate communication from the hand to the eye to the mind. After all, the language of architecture, beyond words themselves, is the laughter of light, proportion, and materiality.

Daniel Libeskind, Daniel Libeskind Architectural Studio

Rendering, Denver Art Museum expansion (Image by Miller Hare, courtesy of the Denver Art Museum)

Rendering, Denver Art Museum expansion
(image by Miller Hare, courtesy of the Denver Art Museum)

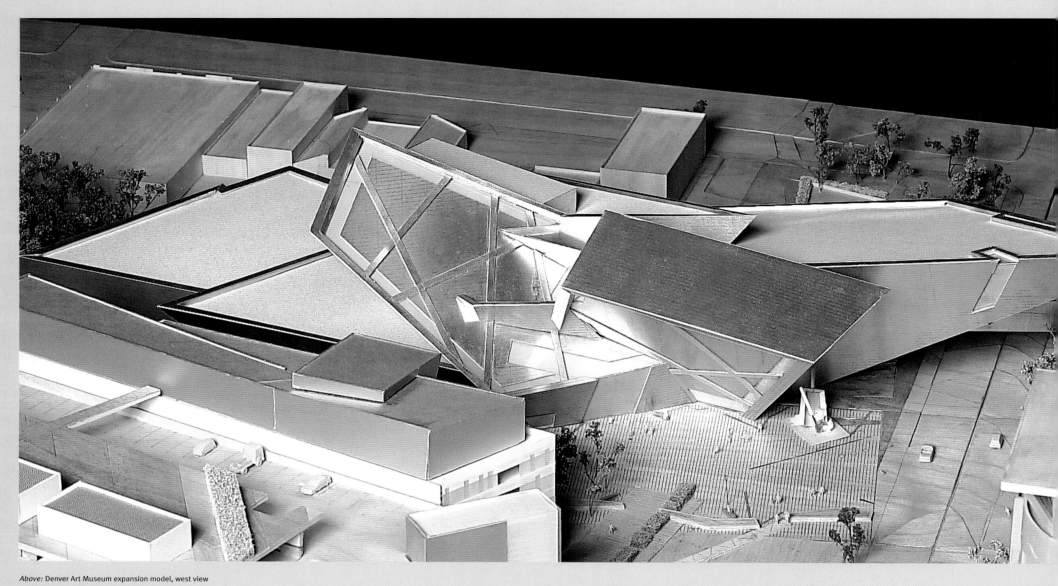

Above: Denver Art Museum expansion model, west view
(photo: courtesy of the Denver Art Museum)
Opposite: Expansion model, showing south view
(photo: courtesy of the Denver Art Museum)

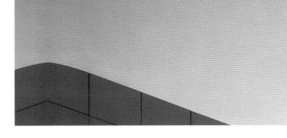

HIGH MUSEUM OF ART ATLANTA, GA

Richard Meier, Renzo Piano

MUSEUM DIRECTOR'S STATEMENT

The High Museum of Art in Atlanta, founded in 1905, continues to expand and evolve as rapidly and profoundly as its hometown. It has distinguished itself as the leading arts institution in the Southeast in terms of its collections, the quality of its special exhibitions and public programming, and its steadily increasing attendance and membership. During the past two decades, the High has experienced unprecedented growth in each of these areas.

▪ The 1983 opening of the critically acclaimed building designed by Richard Meier helped usher in an era of major success for the museum. The award-winning building put the High on the map as one of the nation's most significant cultural institutions and fueled broad public participation in its vast number of programs. Annual attendance has soared to nearly 500,000 visitors per year, with 40 percent of the museum's visitors coming from more than sixty miles away, making the High an economic catalyst for Atlanta.

▪ Our vision is to create a world-class facility that will inspire and delight our audiences and to continue to present significant exhibitions that have great public appeal. We must also expand our education programs to serve even more members of the greater Atlanta community and to bring our diverse audiences together on a common ground, in a welcoming environment

▪ In the past few years, the High has collaborated with major international museums to bring important exhibitions to Atlanta; we have also increased the size and scope of our increasingly comprehensive collection, with a special focus on art specifically relevant to the region. The museum's total holdings include approximately 10,000 works.

▪ After three years of planning, the High Museum selected the renowned architect Renzo Piano to help shape the future of the museum, and he made it possible for us to increase the museum's square footage from 135,000 to 177,000. Piano is known for designing beautiful structures that are sensitive to their setting, as well as wonderful spaces for experiencing art. The new High Museum will serve as a central gathering place or "village green," one that unifies the community. Piano's design will transform the entire Woodruff Arts Center campus into an urban village for the arts, creating great public spaces, a true destination for all of Atlanta.

Michael E. Shapiro

ARCHITECTS' STATEMENTS

The High Museum of Art is a major public building and art repository, which responds to the typological and contextual aspects of the museum's program. The city of Atlanta's progressive building tradition, as well as its role as a developing cultural center, had a strong influence on the design.

▪ The corner site, at the junction of Peachtree and Sixteenth Streets, about two miles from downtown Atlanta, places the museum at an important location for Atlanta's development and within a pedestrian-oriented neighborhood with good public transportation access. The design consists of four quadrants with one carved out, to distinguish it from the other three; the missing quadrant becomes a monumental atrium, the lobby and the ceremonial center of the museum.

▪ The extended ramp is a symbolic gesture reaching out to the street and city, and a foil to the interior ramp, which is the building's chief formal and circulatory element. At the end of the ramp are the main entry and reception area, from which one passes into the four-story atrium. The light-filled atrium space is inspired by, and a commentary on, the central space of the Guggenheim Museum. As in the Guggenheim, the ramp system mediates between the central space and the art itself. In the Guggenheim, however, the ramp doubles as a gallery, whereas in Atlanta, the separation of circulation and gallery space allows the central space to govern the system of movement. This separation also allows the atrium walls to have windows, which admit natural light and offer framed views of the city. The galleries are organized to provide multiple vistas, as well as intimate and large-scale viewing to accommodate the diverse needs of the collection.

▪ Light, whether direct or filtered, admitted through skylights, ribbon glazing, clerestory strips, or minimal perforations in the panel wall, is a consistent preoccupation throughout; apart from its functional aspect, [light] is a symbol of the museum's role as a place of aesthetic illumination and enlightened cultural values. The primary intention of the architecture is to encourage the discovery of these values, and to foster a contemplative appreciation of the museum's collection through its own spatial experience.

Richard Meier, Richard Meier & Partners, Architects

Architecture is not just the art of designing buildings, but the art of telling stories. It is about expressing ideas with building and space.

▪ This new destination will be a campus for art . . . a little city in itself. The buildings will create a campus of culture, and the piazza in the center will be the beginning of the adventure. Here we are creating a sense of life, a sense or urbanity, a sense of intensity.

▪ Every time you have a new scheme, you have to spend time there, you have to understand, you have to catch the genius of the place, because there is always a little genius. Sometimes there are many and nature was one of those little geniuses. The other thing I found fantastic was the presence in the same place of different artistic functions. We started by designing the new additions like building that artistic presence and creating a better unity—incorporating nature. That is when we started to think of a metaphor of a little town or village. It is a place to be, a place where you will feel.

Renzo Piano, Renzo Piano Building Workshop

Main entrance, east façade

CRITIC'S COMMENT ON MEIER BUILDING

The atrium of the High Museum is not a space in which works of art are displayed. It is a monumental space, a grand hall awash in sunlight and shadow from which we can occasionally see a painting or a sculpture poking through from the galleries, but its real purpose is to provide breathing space, a sense of relief from the smaller, more enclosed galleries. It is a room that reminds us that we are in a grandly scaled civic building—something the galleries themselves cannot do if they are to remain properly scaled for the art they contain. . . .
- For the galleries, while not spectacular, are the true heart of this building—they are not an afterthought, a series of leftover spaces into which pictures can be tossed, but seriously conceived rooms, full of an understanding of the needs of art. Richard Meier is one of the few architects practicing today who seems not to be threatened by painting but to love it—and is able, even eager, to enter into a dialogue with it.

Paul Goldberger, *New York Times* (October 5, 1983)

Opposite above: Northwest galleries restored to original Meier design
Opposite below left: Looking east in atrium
Opposite below right: North atrium wall with painting by Sol LeWitt
Left: Lower level of east plaza

Page 210: Circular ramp of atrium
Page 211 above: Multilevel pedestrian ramp in atrium
Page 211 below: Southwest gallery with bar of natural light original to first plans

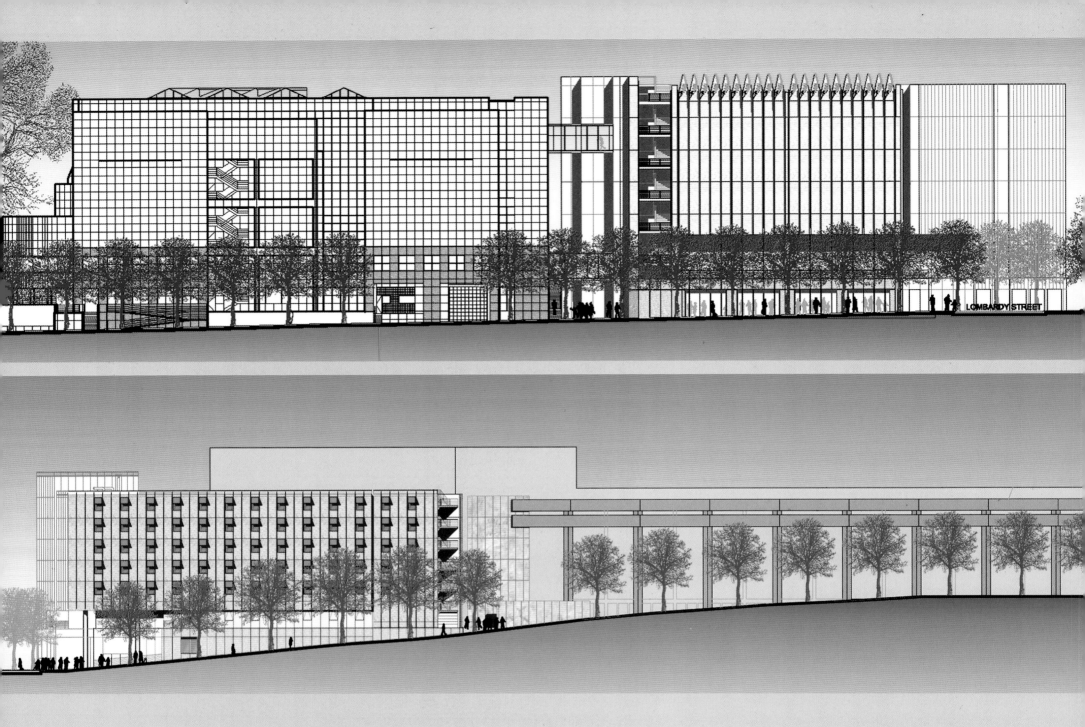

Renderings of addition and remodeling by Renzo Piano
(courtesy of the High Museum of Art)

THE MINNEAPOLIS INSTITUTE OF ARTS MINNEAPOLIS, MN

McKim, Mead and White, Kenzo Tange, Michael Graves

MUSEUM DIRECTOR'S STATEMENT

The Minneapolis Institute of Arts is one of North America's most comprehensive fine-art museums. Its encyclopedic collection of more than 100,000 objects spans five thousand years and represents the world's diverse cultures. With deep roots in the communities it serves, the MIA has a free general-admission policy, an interactive media program, and a recent museum-wide gallery reinstallation project that has delighted local and international audiences. One of Minnesota's preeminent arts organizations, the Minneapolis Institute of Arts reaches more than 700,000 people each year with exciting exhibitions and programs.

■ In 1883 twenty-five citizens of Minneapolis joined together to found the Minneapolis Society of Fine Arts and committed themselves to bringing the arts into the life of their community. Now, more than a century later, the museum they created stands as a monument to this outstanding history of civic involvement and cultural achievement. Since the museum's first building opened its doors in 1915, both it and the collections have changed and grown. The historical architectural design is a Neoclassical landmark in the Twin Cities, designed eighty-five years ago by the noted architectural firm of McKim, Mead and White, and later expanded with additions designed in 1970–74 by Japanese architect Kenzo Tange.

■ The MIA's mission, to bring art and people together, is served by its historic building and parklike grounds. The building currently includes 342,669 square feet for museum operations, and the gallery space devoted to showcasing the permanent collection, special exhibitions, and period rooms totals 121,758 square feet. However, in 2001 the museum determined that it needed expanded space for education, display, and storage. So the search began for a great architectural partner who could adapt a new design to the practical needs of a working museum, with all its specific requirements, within a defined and limited space.

■ The Minneapolis Institute of Arts selected renowned architect Michael Graves to design the building expansion, which will increase the total area by 34 percent, including a 40 percent growth in exhibition space. Graves is also designing the Children's Theatre Company expansion on the same campus as the museum, so there will be harmony between the two projects. Graves's subtle and elegant designs define the essence of classical style produced by a modern master. He has sensitively developed his own vocabulary in this design scheme by respectfully marrying the Neoclassical elegance of the original building with the stark minimalism of Kenzo Tange's addition. The result is a calm and harmonious building well suited to its residential neighborhood.

Evan M. Maurer

ARCHITECT'S STATEMENT

The Minneapolis Institute of Arts occupies a Neoclassical building designed by McKim, Mead and White and completed in 1915. Two modern wings designed by Kenzo Tange were added to the east and west sides of the original building in the 1970s. The eastern wing reoriented the MIA's main entrance from the original building facing Twenty-fourth Street to Third Avenue and incorporated facilities for the Children's Theatre Company. Expansion plans for the MIA and the CTC provide additional space for programs and public services.

■ The four-story, 117,000-square-foot MIA expansion is organized in two sections on the west side of the site facing Stevens Street. A linear addition is located in front of the Tange wing and a square block is located to the south. In addition to increased space for back-of-house functions, the ground floor contains public study rooms for the library and various collections of photography and other works on paper, along with seminar rooms, organized around a central skylighted atrium. The top floor contains a reception hall and preparation space, and the intermediate levels contain galleries connected to renovated space in the existing building. The new space will allow existing space to be reconfigured and the Wells Fargo Collection of Modern Decorative Arts and other collections to be displayed.

■ The design of the new façades addresses both the Neoclassical character of the original building and the abstract modernism of the 1970s additions. Like the McKim, Mead and White building, the composition of the expansion uses rhythm, symmetry, and surface relief to articulate the façades and make the architectural language accessible. Like the Tange additions, the surfaces are simple and unadorned. The light-colored Jura stone used on the face is similar to both and helps unify the appearance of the complex as a whole.

■ Inside the building is a three-story atrium around a circular opening with a domelike lay light on the ceiling. Galleries are simple white rooms. Stone floors are patterned in Jura beige, Jura red-brown, Jura gray-blue, and German greenstone. The public reading rooms and the photo study room are mostly carpeted, with maple millwork. A new maple-paneled reception hall to seat four hundred, located on the top floor, overlooks the Target Garden at the heart of the institute.

Michael Graves, Michael Graves & Associates

McKim, Mead and White north façade

West wing, Tange addition to McKim, Mead and White façade

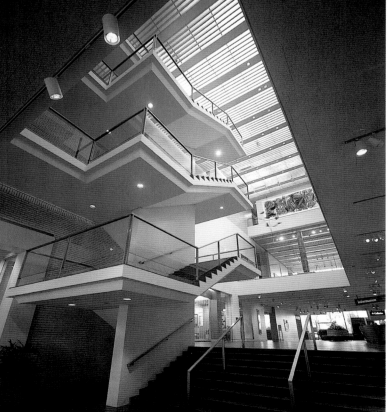

Opposite: Top floor, Ulrich Gallery

Above: View of downtown skyline from third-floor northeast gallery

Left: Entrance-hall atrium

Renderings of addition by Michael Graves (courtesy of Michael Graves & Associates)

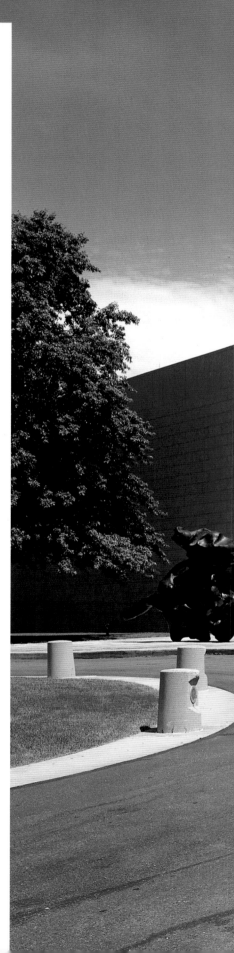

MUSEUM OF FINE ARTS BOSTON, MA

Guy Lowell, Hugh Stubbins, I.M.Pei, Graham Gund, Norman Foster

MUSEUM DIRECTOR'S STATEMENT

The Museum of Fine Arts, Boston (MFA), founded in 1870, is one of the world's great museums. We hold within our walls the height of human achievement. We are an institution with an inspiring history, but also a vigorous and forward-looking philosophy, welcoming visitors from the surrounding community and around the world. Our ultimate goal is to encourage inquiry and heighten public understanding and appreciation of the visual world. With this purpose, the MFA's committed board of trustees determined that a new master site plan for the museum of the twenty-first century was necessary in order to ensure a tradition of providing beautiful gallery settings and gathering spaces.

- In 1999 the MFA commissioned the internationally renowned architectural firm Foster and Partners, UK, to create the first overarching master site plan since the museum's original architect's plan designed by Guy Lowell in 1907. Foster and Partners was selected by the MFA for its analytical abilities, sensitivity to historic buildings, functionally driven designs, and track record in creating buildings of almost symbolic power, which bring new life to their surrounding cities. The partnership between the MFA and Foster and Partners envisages an ambitious transformation of the museum.

- The Master Site Plan is a multiphased project that will dramatically enhance the ways in which visitors navigate the museum's galleries and encounter its great works of art.

- Phase I, the museum's current focus, includes a new wing for the extensive collections of American art and renovated gallery spaces devoted to contemporary and European art. There will also be a glass "jewel box" covering the courtyard at the heart of the museum, as well as improved visitor spaces and amenities. In addition, the facility will provide enhanced conservation and education facilities, augmented climate-control and energy efficiency measures, and strengthened linkage with the surrounding landscape. The designs embody an architectural statement that is not only intensely beautiful, but also innovative and precisely functional. The architects have responded to the needs of the museum, and their designs will stimulate a revitalized visitor experience within the MFA, as well as a greater connection to our neighbors and the city of Boston.

Malcolm Rogers

ARCHITECT'S STATEMENT

It has been tremendously exciting to develop a master site plan for the world-renowned Museum of Fine Arts, Boston. Our inspiration has been drawn from the wealth of the MFA's artistic treasures, its historic Neoclassical architecture and its unique setting amid the urban environment and Frederick Law Olmsted's serene park, the Emerald Necklace. Our aim has been to delicately unite courtyards and galleries both old and new, improving orientation for visitors and strengthening the museum's ties to its surrounding communities.

- More than a building, the MFA is a complex entity that has grown in stages over a very long period of time, and it has become like a city in microcosm.* We have taken stock of the MFA as a composition and analyzed its evolution throughout its extensive building history. We are building on that tradition, striving to rebalance the original master plan developed for the MFA by architect Guy Lowell. We are also examining and melding the interior galleries and the exterior composition, and working toward the wider regeneration of the museum within the historic context of the city of Boston. The use of transparent materials provides many more clues to what is happening behind the museum's façade, in order to make the building more inviting and breaking down the barriers between the private institution and the public domain.

- With a greatly enhanced sense of orientation, visitors will be able to move out from the equivalent of a city square, in this case a glass-covered courtyard, into the new east wing and refurbished and realigned galleries, remaining always aware of their position in relation to the whole museum. The Master Site Plan also creates a new principal level, aligning floors so that moving through the museum will be a much more seamless and graceful experience. A key uniting element is a range of glazed public spaces and glassy top-lit galleries that has been termed the "crystal spine," creating cohesiveness on the MFA's east-to-west axis. This will integrate the courtyard, the new East Wing, new study areas, and galleries, and it will create a social focus, a major public gathering in the heart of the museum, in the heart of a great American city.

Norman Foster, Foster & Partners, UK

* The original Huntington Avenue building was designed in 1907 by Guy Lowell, who made a number of additions in 1909, 1915, 1927, and 1928. The painter John Singer Sargent designed the rotunda and colonnade in 1921 and 1925, and Hugh Stubbins designed two additions in 1968 and 1970. In 1981 I. M. Pei's West Wing was built, and in 1987, Graham Gund was commissioned to renovate and expand the MFA School of Art; an addition to the bookstore and restaurant and a courtyard were designed by Bergmeyer Associates, and in 1999 the garden court and terrace restaurant were built by Jung/Brannen Associates.

South side, main entrance

Above: Eighteenth-century portraits gallery
Right: Tree planting along south façade
Opposite: Main hall through Tom Patti glass wall sculpture

Renderings of addition and remodeling by Norman Foster (courtesy of the Museum of Fine Arts)

MUSEUM OF MODERN ART NEW YORK, NY

Philip Goodwin, Edward Durell Stone, Philip Johnson, Cesar Pelli, Yoshio Taniguchi

MUSEUM DIRECTOR'S STATEMENT

In December 1997, Yoshio Taniguchi's design proposal for the new Museum of Modern Art was selected from a pool of submissions by ten architects. Taniguchi's design offered an elegant concept that would render the important aesthetic, philosophical, and pragmatic issues that face the museum today in the specific language of space, light, and material. The design is the largest building project in the history of the museum—a complete reconfiguration of its midtown Manhattan buildings. The facility will nearly double the size of the museum, adding a restored and enlarged sculpture garden, new gallery spaces, classrooms, lecture hall, theatre, library, and archives, as well as offices, art storage and conservation laboratories, restaurants, and retail spaces.

■ The design is part new construction, part renovation, and part restoration. Instead of designing a single building, Taniguchi recognizes and enhances the fact that the museum is a building composed of many different parts loosely linked together— from Goodwin and Stone's 1939 building to Philip Johnson's many additions, including the Abby Aldrich Rockefeller Sculpture Garden of 1953, and Cesar Pelli's expansion in 1984.

■ Three central issues guided the planning of the institution's expansion. First, the museum is, above all, a place to encounter the singular achievements of modern and contemporary art, and its raison d'être is grounded in the works that form its collection. Second, the museum hopes to create unique experiences that are a result of the engagement of the public with the works of art on display, and to challenge the public's perception of these objects by the ways in which they are presented. The third issue is to organize the museum in a manner that slows down, rather than accelerates, the trajectory of its visitors through the building.

■ The new building is designed to give larger, more flexible galleries for contemporary art and more intimately scaled, architecturally distinctive galleries for modern masterpieces from the collection. Throughout the museum, expansive views of the restored sculpture garden underscore the significance of this urban oasis. A new building devoted to research and education opposite the gallery wing gives concrete form to the museum's dual mission, which is to exhibit the collection and educate the public. Taniguchi's architectural composition reflects an extraordinary understanding of the Museum of Modern Art. As the museum works to simultaneously build its permanent collection, increase its educational initiatives, and encourage a greater understanding of modern art, it only confirms Taniguchi's primary objective—to create an ideal environment for the interaction of people and art.

Glenn D. Lowry

ARCHITECT'S STATEMENT

I approached the plan for the new Museum of Modern Art as if it were an urban design. As opposed to designing a single new building, I treated the museum like a city within a city. Given the existing buildings by Philip Goodwin and Edward Durell Stone, Philip Johnson and Cesar Pelli, the museum's physical campus was already complex. In order to make it more cohesive and organized, I added a strong order to unify the elements by using serene and simple design vocabularies throughout.

■ On Fifty-fourth Street, I emphasized the museum's Sculpture Garden. Its status as the enduring core space of the museum is reinforced by the new backdrop of the uniform façade to the south and the two simple geometric forms on the east and west, accommodating facilities for education and art. Here the synthesis of elements presents a more tranquil composition than on Fifty-third Street, where I have created a collage of milestones in the history of the museum's architecture by restoring or preserving the existing buildings.

■ The new gallery spaces are located in the new building on the western portion of the site. The large temporary-exhibition galleries are placed at the highest public level to take advantage of natural illumination from skylights, and the gallery dedicated to contemporary art is closest to street level, in order to give prominence to the presentation of new art.

■ As the Sculpture Garden is the core of the exterior space, I added a six-story skylighted atrium to act as the core of the new expansion project. The galleries, organized around the atrium, are connected by multilevel bridges, which serve to orient visitors to all levels. From the bridges, one can experience the dynamic space that links the two core spaces both visually and physically.

■ My intention was to create an environment for people and art, not just a physical building. A useful analogy to illustrate this premise is the Japanese tea ceremony. The teacup is very simple in form and very subdued in expression. But once the tea is poured, the teacup is transformed into a whole new object. It is not the object alone that is important, but the totality—the temperature of the tea, its color, and its aroma. In the museum, my fundamental concern in the choice of materials, in the interplay of natural light, and in refining the proportions of the interrelated elements, was to create a place where the architecture itself remains quiet and the environment is paramount.

Yoshio Taniguchi

Renderings of addition and remodeling by Masanori Ka Sahara and Taniguchi and Associates (courtesy The Museum of Modern Art)

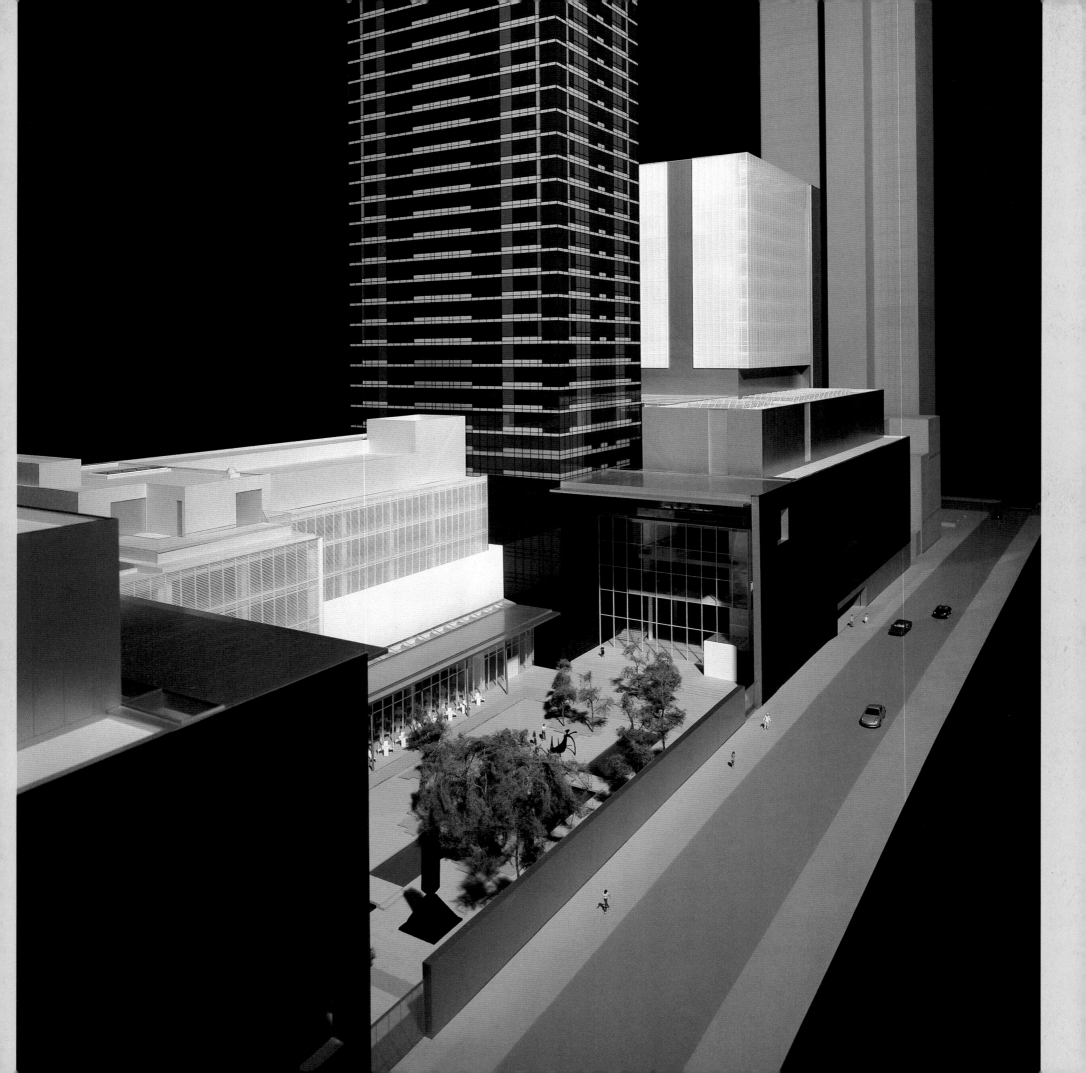

WALKER ART CENTER MINNEAPOLIS, MI

Edward Larrabee Barnes, Jacques Herzog/Pierre de Meuron

Hennepin elevation by day and by night (images © Herzog & de Meuron)

Opposite: Close-ups of building exterior (image ©Herzog & de Meuron)

Above: Hennepin lounge (image ©Herzog & de Meuron)